# LIVING LITURGY™

## FOR
## CANTORS

# LIVING LITURGY™

## FOR
## CANTORS

### Year B • 2015

*Kathleen Harmon, S.N.D. de N.*
*Joyce Ann Zimmerman, C.PP.S.*
*Rev. John W. Tonkin*

**LITURGICAL PRESS**
Collegeville, Minnesota

www.litpress.org

# Presented to

_____

*in grateful appreciation*
*for ministering as a Cantor*

_____

_____

*(date)*

# USING THIS RESOURCE

*Living Liturgy™ for Cantors* is intended to help psalmists prepare themselves to sing the responsorial psalm by reflecting on the text of the psalm in the context of the readings of the day and applying this reflection to a spirituality for daily living. A cantor who has a sense of how the psalm is connected to the readings and to his or her daily living will sing the psalm with greater sensitivity. The cantor's singing will flow out of personal encounter with God, who works through the Liturgy of the Word to draw the cantor and the assembly more fully into being who they are: the Body of Christ.

*Living Liturgy™ for Cantors* contains the gospel readings, first readings, and responsorial psalms for every Sunday of the liturgical year, for those solemnities that are holy days of obligation, and for Ash Wednesday. An appendix contains the second readings for those days (namely, the Sundays of Advent, Christmas, Lent, and Easter; the solemnities; and Ash Wednesday) when that reading has an intended connection to the other readings. For each Sunday or solemnity the book provides a brief reflection on the gospel, a section connecting the psalm to the readings, a suggestion to help the psalmist prepare spiritually to sing the psalm, and a prayer drawn from the readings and the psalm.

While this book is a small one, it offers a wealth of preparatory material for the cantor of the psalm. Cantors might find the following method helpful in using this book and should feel free to adapt the method or to create another one to suit their needs and situation.

On Monday, read the gospel and spend some time reflecting on its meaning. Ask yourself who Jesus is in this gospel and what he is saying or doing. Who are we, and what are we saying or doing?

On Tuesday, read the first reading. Ask yourself who God is in this reading and what God is saying or doing. Who are we, and what are we saying or doing? Read "Reflecting on Living the Gospel" and see what further insights open up for you.

On Wednesday, look at the text of the psalm and see how it is connected to the readings. During the festal seasons of Advent, Christmas, Lent, and Easter, and for those days that are solemnities, read the second reading.

On Thursday, read "Connecting the Responsorial Psalm to the Readings" and "Psalmist Preparation" and decide how you might implement the suggested spirituality.

On Friday, sing through the psalm, letting your reflection and your daily living add a new dimension to your understanding of the text. Pray the suggested prayer and ask for the grace to do your ministry well.

On Saturday and Sunday, give yourself over to Christ so that he may be the voice the assembly hears.

Even more important than musical preparation of the psalm setting is the cantor's prayerful reflection on the meaning of the text and its role in his or her daily living. The cantor who does this kind of preparation discovers that his or her singing is a dialogue with God that mirrors the dialogue going on between God and the assembly in the Liturgy of the Word. A dimension opens up in the cantor's singing that is far deeper than the beauty of his or her voice. What the assembly hears is the cantor's surrender of self to the paschal mystery of Christ, and it is this surrender to which they respond.

**Gospel (Mark 13:33-37; L2B)**

Jesus said to his disciples: "Be watchful! Be alert! You do not know when the time will come. It is like a man traveling abroad. He leaves home and places his servants in charge, each with his own work, and orders the gatekeeper to be on the watch. Watch, therefore; you do not know when the lord of the house is coming, whether in the evening, or at midnight, or at cockcrow, or in the morning. May he not come suddenly and find you sleeping. What I say to you, I say to all: 'Watch!'"

**First Reading (Isa 63:16b-17, 19b; 64:2-7)**

You, LORD, are our father,
    our redeemer you are named forever.
Why do you let us wander, O LORD, from your ways,
    and harden our hearts so that we fear you not?
Return for the sake of your servants,
    the tribes of your heritage.
Oh, that you would rend the heavens and come down,
    with the mountains quaking before you,
While you wrought awesome deeds we could not hope for,
    such as they had not heard of from of old.
No ear has ever heard, no eye ever seen, any God but you
    doing such deeds for those who wait for him.
Would that you might meet us doing right,
    that we were mindful of you in our ways!
Behold, you are angry, and we are sinful;
    all of us have become like unclean people,
    all our good deeds are like polluted rags;
We have all withered like leaves,
    and our guilt carries us away like the wind.
There is none who calls upon your name,
    who rouses himself to cling to you;
For you have hidden your face from us
    and have delivered us up to our guilt.

Yet, O LORD, you are our father;
we are the clay and you the potter:
we are all the work of your hands.

**Responsorial Psalm (Ps 80:2-3, 15-16, 18-19)**

℟. (4) Lord, make us turn to you; let us see your face and we shall
be saved.

O shepherd of Israel, hearken,
from your throne upon the cherubim, shine forth.
Rouse your power,
and come to save us.

℟. Lord, make us turn to you; let us see your face and we shall
be saved.

Once again, O LORD of hosts,
look down from heaven, and see;
take care of this vine,
and protect what your right hand has planted,
the son of man whom you yourself made strong.

℟. Lord, make us turn to you; let us see your face and we shall
be saved.

May your help be with the man of your right hand,
with the son of man whom you yourself made strong.
Then we will no more withdraw from you;
give us new life, and we will call upon your name.

℟. Lord, make us turn to you; let us see your face and we shall
be saved.

*See Appendix, p. 199, for Second Reading*

### Reflecting on Living the Gospel

Four times in this gospel Christ commands us, "Be watchful!" or
"Watch!" Being watchful and alert for the Second Coming is not enough;
we must consciously seek to identify Christ already present *now.* If we
are proactively watching for everyday encounters with Christ, he will
surely not find us "sleeping," neither now nor when he returns. The Second Coming becomes real for us in our encounters with Christ in the here
and now.

9

**Connecting the Responsorial Psalm to the Readings**

Psalm 80 was written at a time when Israel had suffered devastating defeat at the hands of an enemy. Their homeland lay in ruins, their way of life destroyed. In anguish they cried out to God. The "man of your right hand" they prayed for in verse 18 was the king who embodied God's presence among them. By restoring the king's strength God would restore Israel's identity and way of life.

In numerous ways, Israel had withdrawn from God, and their guilt was carrying them away (first reading). In the psalm, Israel begs God: "make us turn to you" that we may be saved. On this First Sunday of Advent, this psalm is our call from our own time and situation. How have we wandered from God's ways (first reading)? How are we in need of redemption? The second reading reminds us the redemption we seek has been granted in Christ. Like gatekeepers, then, we must watch diligently for his return (gospel), for when we see his face we will be saved (psalm refrain).

**Psalmist Preparation**

As you prepare to sing this psalm, pray about where in your life you need God to turn you around so that you may see God's face more clearly. How have you wandered from God's ways? What is God doing to bring you back? How is turning back to God part of the work of Advent?

**Prayer**

God of our expectations, turn your face toward us that the light of your mercy and the glory of your salvation may lead us back from our wandering ways to the fullness of life you offer us in Christ Jesus your Son. We ask this in his name. Amen.

### Gospel (Mark 1:1-8; L5B)

The beginning of the Gospel of Jesus Christ the Son of God.

As it is written in Isaiah the prophet:

> *Behold, I am sending my messenger*
> *ahead of you;*
> *he will prepare your way.*
> *A voice of one crying out in the desert:*
> *"Prepare the way of the Lord,*
> *make straight his paths."*

John the Baptist appeared in the desert proclaiming a baptism of repentance for the forgiveness of sins. People of the whole Judean countryside and all the inhabitants of Jerusalem were going out to him and were being baptized by him in the Jordan River as they acknowledged their sins. John was clothed in camel's hair, with a leather belt around his waist. He fed on locusts and wild honey. And this is what he proclaimed: "One mightier than I is coming after me. I am not worthy to stoop and loosen the thongs of his sandals. I have baptized you with water; he will baptize you with the Holy Spirit."

### First Reading (Isa 40:1-5, 9-11)

> Comfort, give comfort to my people,
> says your God.
> Speak tenderly to Jerusalem, and proclaim to her
> that her service is at an end,
> her guilt is expiated;
> Indeed, she has received from the hand of the LORD
> double for all her sins.
>
> A voice cries out:
> In the desert prepare the way of the LORD!
> Make straight in the wasteland a highway for our God!
> Every valley shall be filled in,
> every mountain and hill shall be made low;
> The rugged land shall be made a plain,
> the rough country, a broad valley.
> Then the glory of the LORD shall be revealed,

and all people shall see it together;
for the mouth of the LORD has spoken.

Go up on to a high mountain,
  Zion, herald of glad tidings;
Cry out at the top of your voice,
  Jerusalem, herald of good news!
Fear not to cry out
  and say to the cities of Judah:
  Here is your God!
Here comes with power
  the Lord GOD,
  who rules by his strong arm;
Here is his reward with him,
  his recompense before him.
Like a shepherd he feeds his flock;
  in his arms he gathers the lambs,
Carrying them in his bosom,
  and leading the ewes with care.

**Responsorial Psalm (Ps 85:9-10, 11-12, 13-14)**

R̶. (8) Lord, let us see your kindness, and grant us your salvation.

I will hear what God proclaims;
  the LORD—for he proclaims peace to his people.
Near indeed is his salvation to those who fear him,
  glory dwelling in our land.

R̶. Lord, let us see your kindness, and grant us your salvation.

Kindness and truth shall meet;
  justice and peace shall kiss.
Truth shall spring out of the earth,
  and justice shall look down from heaven.

R̶. Lord, let us see your kindness, and grant us your salvation.

The LORD himself will give his benefits;
  our land shall yield its increase.
Justice shall walk before him,
  and prepare the way of his steps.

R̶. Lord, let us see your kindness, and grant us your salvation.

*See Appendix, p. 199, for Second Reading*

### Reflecting on Living the Gospel

John was a desert ascetic whose mission was to prepare the people for a life-transforming change—the Lord is coming! Who is this Lord? One mightier than John. How so? John announces the nearness of salvation; Jesus *is* the salvation. John baptizes with water, Jesus with the Holy Spirit. What does this mean? Jesus' baptism instills God's very Life through the power of the Holy Spirit within us. Baptism with the Holy Spirit transforms our preparation into fulfillment—the Lord has come!

### Connecting the Responsorial Psalm to the Readings

A new day is coming when salvation (psalm) will replace sin and servitude (first reading), when God will come with power (first reading) and peace (psalm). A new person is coming, the One who will baptize with the Holy Spirit (gospel). God's own justice will prepare the way (psalm). But so are we to prepare the way (gospel, first reading). We who have been baptized in the Holy Spirit are to be persons of "holiness and devotion" (second reading) whose manner of living heralds the kindness, peace, truth, and justice (psalm) of the new heavens and new earth we so eagerly await (second reading).

### Psalmist Preparation

How is this psalm a proclamation of the "new heavens and a new earth" God is promising? How through baptism have you already been made part of this new creation by the Holy Spirit? How can your singing of this psalm both announce what has already happened and call the people to prepare for what is yet to come?

### Prayer

Saving God, in you kindness and truth meet, justice and peace kiss. Make your justice our path and your truth our word that all people may come to know the salvation you offer. We ask this through Christ our Lord. Amen.

### Gospel (Luke 1:26-38; L689)

The angel Gabriel was sent from God to a town of Galilee called Nazareth, to a virgin betrothed to a man named Joseph, of the house of David, and the virgin's name was Mary. And coming to her, he said, "Hail, full of grace! The Lord is with you." But she was greatly troubled at what was said and pondered what sort of greeting this might be. Then the angel said to her, "Do not be afraid, Mary, for you have found favor with God. Behold, you will conceive in your womb and bear a son, and you shall name him Jesus. He will be great and will be called Son of the Most High, and the Lord God will give him the throne of David his father, and he will rule over the house of Jacob forever, and of his Kingdom there will be no end." But Mary said to the angel, "How can this be, since I have no relations with a man?" And the angel said to her in reply, "The Holy Spirit will come upon you, and the power of the Most High will overshadow you. Therefore the child to be born will be called holy, the Son of God. And behold, Elizabeth, your relative, has also conceived a son in her old age, and this is the sixth month for her who was called barren; for nothing will be impossible for God." Mary said, "Behold, I am the handmaid of the Lord. May it be done to me according to your word." Then the angel departed from her.

### First Reading (Gen 3:9-15, 20)

After the man, Adam, had eaten of the tree, the LORD God called to the man and asked him, "Where are you?" He answered, "I heard you in the garden; but I was afraid, because I was naked, so I hid myself." Then he asked, "Who told you that you were naked? You have eaten, then, from the tree of which I had forbidden you to eat!" The man replied, "The woman whom you put here with me— she gave me fruit from the tree, and so I ate it." The LORD God then asked the woman, "Why did you do such a thing?" The woman answered, "The serpent tricked me into it, so I ate it."

Then the LORD God said to the serpent:

"Because you have done this, you shall be banned
    from all the animals
    and from all the wild creatures;
on your belly shall you crawl,
    and dirt shall you eat
    all the days of your life.
I will put enmity between you and the woman,
    and between your offspring and hers;
he will strike at your head,
    while you strike at his heel."

The man called his wife Eve, because she became the mother of all the living.

### Responsorial Psalm (Ps 98:1, 2-3, 3-4)

R︠. (1a) Sing to the Lord a new song, for he has done marvelous deeds.

Sing to the LORD a new song,
    for he has done wondrous deeds;
his right hand has won victory for him,
    his holy arm.

R︠. Sing to the Lord a new song, for he has done marvelous deeds.

The LORD has made his salvation known:
    in the sight of the nations he has revealed his justice.
He has remembered his kindness and his faithfulness
    toward the house of Israel.

R︠. Sing to the Lord a new song, for he has done marvelous deeds.

All the ends of the earth have seen
    the salvation by our God.
Sing joyfully to the LORD, all you lands;
    break into song; sing praise.

R︠. Sing to the Lord a new song, for he has done marvelous deeds.

*See Appendix, p. 199, for Second Reading*

# THE IMMACULATE CONCEPTION OF THE BLESSED VIRGIN MARY

### Reflecting on Living the Gospel

Even before assenting to conceiving Jesus by the Holy Spirit, Mary had made "May it be done to me" the abiding habit of her way of relating to God and choosing to do God's will. The relationship between Mary and God had grown all her life to the point where her yes was simply the natural thing for her to do. It didn't take thinking; it was an answer of the heart. So must our yes to God be an answer of the heart.

### Connecting the Responsorial Psalm to the Readings

For the solemnity of the Immaculate Conception this year we sing the same responsorial psalm we will sing on Christmas Day (Psalm 98). On the solemnity the refrain is drawn from Mary's own words in her *Magnificat*, "The Mighty One has done great things for me" (Luke 1:49). Adam and Eve's loss of grace in the garden (first reading) is completely reversed in the person of Mary, who is "full of grace" (gospel). But God's marvelous deeds do not end with her. We, too, have been chosen in Christ for wondrous things (second reading). And so we sing this psalm of praise with Mary, knowing that we, too, have been favored by God and filled with grace.

### Psalmist Preparation

In this psalm you sing about the "marvelous deeds" God accomplished in Mary, and also about the wondrous works God accomplishes in every human person. As you prepare to sing this psalm, spend some time looking for God's marvelous deeds of salvation—within yourself, within your family, within the church—and give God praise.

### Prayer

God of glory, just as you chose Mary to be full of grace, so have you chosen us to be holy and blameless before you. May we, like Mary, always say yes to your call so that all the ends of the earth may know your salvation and sing your praise. We ask this through Christ our Lord. Amen.

**Gospel (John 1:6-8, 19-28; L8B)**

A man named John was sent from God. He came for testimony, to testify to the light, so that all might believe through him. He was not the light, but came to testify to the light.

And this is the testimony of John. When the Jews from Jerusalem sent priests and Levites to him to ask him, "Who are you?" he admitted and did not deny it, but admitted, "I am not the Christ." So they asked him, "What are you then? Are you Elijah?" And he said, "I am not." "Are you the Prophet?" He answered, "No." So they said to him, "Who are you, so we can give an answer to those who sent us? What do you have to say for yourself?" He said:

"I am *the voice of one crying out in the desert,*
*make straight the way of the Lord,*

as Isaiah the prophet said." Some Pharisees were also sent. They asked him, "Why then do you baptize if you are not the Christ or Elijah or the Prophet?" John answered them, "I baptize with water; but there is one among you whom you do not recognize, the one who is coming after me, whose sandal strap I am not worthy to untie." This happened in Bethany across the Jordan, where John was baptizing.

**First Reading (Isa 61:1-2a, 10-11)**

The spirit of the Lord God is upon me,
    because the Lord has anointed me;
He has sent me to bring glad tidings to the poor,
    to heal the brokenhearted,
To proclaim liberty to the captives
    and release to the prisoners,
To announce a year of favor from the Lord
    and a day of vindication by our God.

I rejoice heartily in the Lord,
    in my God is the joy of my soul;

For he has clothed me with a robe of salvation
and wrapped me in a mantle of justice,
Like a bridegroom adorned with a diadem,
like a bride bedecked with her jewels.
As the earth brings forth its plants,
and a garden makes its growth spring up,
So will the Lord GOD make justice and praise
spring up before all the nations.

### Responsorial Psalm (Luke 1:46-48, 49-50, 53-54)

R℣. (Isa 61:10b) My soul rejoices in my God.

My soul proclaims the greatness of the Lord;
my spirit rejoices in God my Savior,
for he has looked upon his lowly servant.
From this day all generations will call me blessed:

R℣. My soul rejoices in my God.

The Almighty has done great things for me,
and holy is his Name.
He has mercy on those who fear him
in every generation.

R℣. My soul rejoices in my God.

He has filled the hungry with good things,
and the rich he has sent away empty.
He has come to the help of his servant Israel
for he has remembered his promise of mercy.

R℣. My soul rejoices in my God.

*See Appendix, p. 199, for Second Reading*

### Reflecting on Living the Gospel

After saying clearly who he is not ("Christ or Elijah or the Prophet"),
John does say who he is: "I am the voice of one crying out in the desert."
"Voice": the audible revelation of self. "Crying out": testifying to core
convictions. "Desert": place of barrenness and desolation as well as a
place of testing and growth. So who is John? The one who in his very
being recognizes the Christ who has come to lead the people into the fullness of light and Life.

### Connecting the Responsorial Psalm to the Readings

This Sunday's responsorial psalm is taken from the *Magnificat*, Mary's hymn of praise for what God is doing for her and for all people. Mary testifies to the presence and activity of God within her and within the world. What she sees God doing is concrete: the lowly are being lifted up, the hungry are being filled, mercy is being granted. Like John the Baptist, Mary knew who she was (God's "lowly servant") and who God was (the Almighty who does "great things"). She cannot hold herself back from proclaiming what she knows. She must announce the "glad tidings" of salvation (first reading). As we sing her song, we, too, proclaim who God is and what God is doing. We, too, rejoice in announcing salvation.

### Psalmist Preparation

As you sing these verses from the *Magnificat*, Mary's words become your words. With Mary, you take up the mission of John the Baptist (gospel) and of Isaiah (first reading). You announce the coming of the Savior and the presence of salvation. Do you believe what you announce?

### Prayer

Great and glorious God, you remember your promise of mercy toward those who hunger for salvation. May we, like Mary, rejoice in you always and proclaim your greatness to all the world. We ask this through Christ our Lord. Amen.

### Gospel (Luke 1:26-38; L I I B)

The angel Gabriel was sent from God to a town of Galilee called Nazareth, to a virgin betrothed to a man named Joseph, of the house of David, and the virgin's name was Mary. And coming to her, he said, "Hail, full of grace! The Lord is with you." But she was greatly troubled at what was said and pondered what sort of greeting this might be. Then the angel said to her, "Do not be afraid, Mary, for you have found favor with God.

"Behold, you will conceive in your womb and bear a son, and you shall name him Jesus. He will be great and will be called Son of the Most High, and the Lord God will give him the throne of David his father, and he will rule over the house of Jacob forever, and of his kingdom there will be no end." But Mary said to the angel, "How can this be, since I have no relations with a man?" And the angel said to her in reply, "The Holy Spirit will come upon you, and the power of the Most High will overshadow you. Therefore the child to be born will be called holy, the Son of God. And behold, Elizabeth, your relative, has also conceived a son in her old age, and this is the sixth month for her who was called barren; for nothing will be impossible for God." Mary said, "Behold, I am the handmaid of the Lord. May it be done to me according to your word." Then the angel departed from her.

### First Reading (2 Sam 7:1-5, 8b-12, 14a, 16)

When King David was settled in his palace, and the LORD had given him rest from his enemies on every side, he said to Nathan the prophet, "Here I am living in a house of cedar, while the ark of God dwells in a tent!" Nathan answered the king, "Go, do whatever you have in mind, for the LORD is with you." But that night the LORD spoke to Nathan and said: "Go, tell my servant David, 'Thus says the LORD: Should you build me a house to dwell in?

"'It was I who took you from the pasture and from the care of the flock to be commander of my people Israel. I have been with you wherever you went, and I have destroyed all your enemies before you. And I will make you famous like the great ones of the earth. I will fix a place for my people Israel; I will plant them so that they may dwell in their place without further disturbance. Neither shall the wicked continue to afflict them as they did of old, since the time I first appointed judges over my people Israel. I will give you rest from all your enemies. The LORD also reveals to you that he will establish a house for you. And when your time comes and you rest with your ancestors, I will raise up your heir after you, sprung from your loins, and I will make his kingdom firm. I will be a father to him, and he shall be a son to me. Your house and your kingdom shall endure forever before me; your throne shall stand firm forever.'"

***Responsorial Psalm* (Ps 89:2-3, 4-5, 27, 29)**

℟. (2a) Forever I will sing the goodness of the Lord.

The promises of the LORD I will sing forever;
 through all generations my mouth shall proclaim your faithfulness.
For you have said, "My kindness is established forever";
 in heaven you have confirmed your faithfulness.

℟. Forever I will sing the goodness of the Lord.

"I have made a covenant with my chosen one,
 I have sworn to David my servant:
Forever will I confirm your posterity
 and establish your throne for all generations."

℟. Forever I will sing the goodness of the Lord.

"He shall say of me, 'You are my father,
 my God, the Rock, my savior.'
Forever I will maintain my kindness toward him,
 and my covenant with him stands firm."

℟. Forever I will sing the goodness of the Lord.

*See Appendix, p. 200, for Second Reading*

***Reflecting on Living the Gospel***

God's whole plan of salvation is a perpetual annunciation. In this gospel, there are numerous "annunciations" beyond Gabriel's revealing to Mary that she would conceive "the Son of God." Gabriel makes known that Mary is holy; that the child shall be named Jesus; that the kingdom of this Child would have no end; that this Child is "holy, the Son of God"; that Elizabeth has conceived; that "nothing will be impossible for God"; and that Mary is God's faithful and obedient handmaid. Indeed, perpetual annunciation is God's pattern of relating to us.

### Connecting the Responsorial Psalm to the Readings

The verses of this Sunday's responsorial psalm are taken from a lengthy psalm telling a painful story of what seems to be infidelity on God's part. Psalm 89 begins with God promising David everlasting love and loyalty. David's throne, God swears, will stand forever. No matter what, God promises, I will never withdraw my love. When David's kingdom is ultimately destroyed, then, the people cry out, "Where are your former mercies, Lord?" (v. 50).

The Lectionary uses verses from Psalm 89 that declare God's love and fidelity to David. The selections are awkward to sing, however, because sometimes the psalmist speaks to God, sometimes God speaks to the psalmist, and in the refrain the assembly speaks to the world. It is the re-frain which is the key liturgically to what we sing about in these verses. No matter what happens in history God's care for us is steadfast. Despite appearances to the contrary, God remains faithful to the divine promise. We can sing "forever" of "the goodness of the Lord" (psalm refrain) be-cause the Lord is with us and our Savior is being born among us (gospel).

### Psalmist Preparation

In preparing to sing this responsorial psalm you need to pay careful at-tention to the shifts in direct address which the verses contain. When are you speaking *to* God? When are you speaking *for* God? Your task will be to communicate both God's love for us and our love for God. How might you do this?

### Prayer

God of the covenant, your promise to us lasts for all eternity. Open our eyes to see your saving deeds and our lips to sing of your goodness to all whom we meet. We ask this through Christ our Lord. Amen.

**DECEMBER 24, 2014**

**Gospel (Matt 1:1-25 [or Matt 1:18-25]; L13 ABC)**

The book of the genealogy of Jesus Christ, the son of David, the son of Abraham.

Abraham became the father of Isaac, Isaac the father of Jacob, Jacob the father of Judah and his brothers. Judah became the father of Perez and Zerah, whose mother was Tamar. Perez became the father of Hezron, Hezron the father of Ram, Ram the father of Amminadab. Amminadab became the father of Nahshon, Nahshon the father of Salmon, Salmon the father of Boaz, whose mother was Rahab. Boaz became the father of Obed, whose mother was Ruth. Obed became the father of Jesse, Jesse the father of David the king.

David became the father of Solomon, whose mother had been the wife of Uriah. Solomon became the father of Rehoboam, Rehoboam the father of Abijah, Abijah the father of Asaph. Asaph became the father of Jehoshaphat, Jehoshaphat the father of Joram, Joram the father of Uzziah. Uzziah became the father of Jotham, Jotham the father of Ahaz, Ahaz the father of Hezekiah. Hezekiah became the father of Manasseh, Manasseh the father of Amos, Amos the father of Josiah. Josiah became the father of Jechoniah and his brothers at the time of the Babylonian exile.

After the Babylonian exile, Jechoniah became the father of Shealtiel, Shealtiel the father of Zerubbabel, Zerubbabel the father of Abiud. Abiud became the father of Eliakim, Eliakim the father of Azor, Azor the father of Zadok. Zadok became the father of Achim, Achim the father of Eliud, Eliud the father of Eleazar. Eleazar became the father of Matthan, Matthan the father of Jacob, Jacob the father of Joseph, the husband of Mary. Of her was born Jesus who is called the Christ.

Thus the total number of generations from Abraham to David is fourteen generations; from David to the Babylonian exile, fourteen generations; from the Babylonian exile to the Christ, fourteen generations.

[Now this is how the birth of Jesus Christ came about. When his mother Mary was betrothed to Joseph, but before they lived together, she was found with child through the Holy Spirit. Joseph her husband, since he was a righteous man, yet unwilling to expose her to shame, decided to divorce her quietly. Such was his intention when, behold, the angel of the Lord appeared to him in a dream and said, "Joseph, son of David, do not be afraid to take Mary your wife into your home. For it is through the Holy Spirit that this child has been conceived in her. She will bear a son and you are to name him Jesus, because he will save his people from their sins." All this took place to fulfill what the Lord had said through the prophet:

> Behold, the virgin shall conceive and bear a son,
>   and they shall name him Emmanuel,

which means "God is with us." When Joseph awoke, he did as the angel of the Lord had commanded him and took his wife into his home. He had no relations with her until she bore a son, and he named him Jesus.]

### First Reading (Isa 62:1-5)

For Zion's sake I will not be silent,
    for Jerusalem's sake I will not be quiet,
until her vindication shines forth like the dawn
    and her victory like a burning torch.

Nations shall behold your vindication,
    and all the kings your glory;
you shall be called by a new name
    pronounced by the mouth of the LORD.
You shall be a glorious crown in the hand of the LORD,
    a royal diadem held by your God.
No more shall people call you "Forsaken,"
    or your land "Desolate,"
but you shall be called "My Delight,"
    and your land "Espoused."
For the LORD delights in you
    and makes your land his spouse.
As a young man marries a virgin,
    your Builder shall marry you;
and as a bridegroom rejoices in his bride
    so shall your God rejoice in you.

*Responsorial Psalm* **(Ps 89:4-5, 16-17, 27, 29)**

℟. (2a) Forever I will sing the goodness of the Lord.

I have made a covenant with my chosen one,
   I have sworn to David my servant:
forever will I confirm your posterity
   and establish your throne for all generations.

℟. Forever I will sing the goodness of the Lord.

Blessed the people who know the joyful shout;
   in the light of your countenance, O LORD, they walk.
At your name they rejoice all the day,
   and through your justice they are exalted.

℟. Forever I will sing the goodness of the Lord.

He shall say of me, "You are my father,
   my God, the Rock, my savior."
Forever I will maintain my kindness toward him,
   and my covenant with him stands firm.

℟. Forever I will sing the goodness of the Lord.

*See Appendix, p. 200, for Second Reading*

### Reflecting on Living the Gospel

Joseph models for us what it means to be in right relationship with God. He wishes to keep the law, but does not want his beloved betrothed to be shamed; he hears the word of God from the angel, and obeys by taking Mary as his wife and naming her Son Jesus. By listening to God and changing his mind (and his course of life), Joseph is a righteous servant of God who directly cooperates in God's saving work.

### Connecting the Responsorial Psalm to the Readings

In the first reading for the Christmas Vigil Mass God promises to keep acting until salvation is completed. In the second reading Paul expounds how God has relentlessly acted throughout history for this salvation. With its lengthy genealogy the gospel grounds progress toward salvation in real human history, among real human beings. Although this salvation has been long in coming, its coming has been nonetheless certain thanks to the promise of God given in covenant fidelity (responsorial psalm) and spousal love (first reading). As we anticipate tomorrow the full celebration of the birth of Christ we stand with generations who looked forward to this day. May we with them and with Mary and Joseph perceive in ordinary human events the in-breaking of divine miracle. May we stand with them among the blessed who see and sing of "the goodness of the Lord."

### Psalmist Preparation

In this responsorial psalm you sing of the covenant made by God with "my chosen one." Do you recognize yourself as "chosen" by God, as participating in the covenant God made with Israel, David, Mary and Joseph? Do you recognize the assembly as "chosen"? How might this awareness affect your singing of this psalm and your celebration of Christmas?

### Prayer

God of salvation, in the fullness of time you sent your Son to be with us in human flesh. May we live always as your children, faithful to your covenant and singing of your goodness. We ask this in his name. Amen.

**DECEMBER 25, 2014**

### Gospel (Luke 2:1-14; L14ABC)

In those days a decree went out from Caesar Augustus that the whole world should be enrolled. This was the first enrollment, when Quirinius was governor of Syria. So all went to be enrolled, each to his own town. And Joseph too went up from Galilee from the town of Nazareth to Judea, to the city of David that is called Bethlehem, because he was of the house and family of David, to be enrolled with Mary, his betrothed, who was with child. While they were there, the time came for her to have her child, and she gave birth to her firstborn son. She wrapped him in swaddling clothes and laid him in a manger, because there was no room for them in the inn.

Now there were shepherds in that region living in the fields and keeping the night watch over their flock. The angel of the Lord appeared to them and the glory of the Lord shone around them, and they were struck with great fear. The angel said to them, "Do not be afraid; for behold, I proclaim to you good news of great joy that will be for all the people. For today in the city of David a savior has been born for you who is Christ and Lord. And this will be a sign for you: you will find an infant wrapped in swaddling clothes and lying in a manger." And suddenly there was a multitude of the heavenly host with the angel, praising God and saying:

"Glory to God in the highest
and on earth peace to those on whom his favor rests."

### First Reading (Isa 9:1-6)

The people who walked in darkness
have seen a great light;
upon those who dwelt in the land of gloom
a light has shone.
You have brought them abundant joy
and great rejoicing,
as they rejoice before you as at the harvest,
as people make merry when dividing spoils.

For the yoke that burdened them,
    the pole on their shoulder,
and the rod of their taskmaster
    you have smashed, as on the day of Midian.
For every boot that tramped in battle,
    every cloak rolled in blood,
    will be burned as fuel for flames.
For a child is born to us, a son is given us;
    upon his shoulder dominion rests.
They name him Wonder-Counselor, God-Hero,
    Father-Forever, Prince of Peace.
His dominion is vast
    and forever peaceful,
from David's throne, and over his kingdom,
    which he confirms and sustains
by judgment and justice,
    both now and forever.
The zeal of the LORD of hosts will do this!

### Responsorial Psalm (Ps 96:1-2, 2-3, 11-12, 13)

R℣. (Luke 2:11) Today is born our Savior, Christ the Lord.

Sing to the LORD a new song;
    sing to the LORD, all you lands.
Sing to the LORD; bless his name.

R℣. Today is born our Savior, Christ the Lord.

Announce his salvation, day after day.
    Tell his glory among the nations;
    among all peoples, his wondrous deeds.

R℣. Today is born our Savior, Christ the Lord.

Let the heavens be glad and the earth rejoice;
    let the sea and what fills it resound;
    let the plains be joyful and all that is in them!
Then shall all the trees of the forest exult.

R℣. Today is born our Savior, Christ the Lord.

They shall exult before the Lord, for he comes;
   for he comes to rule the earth.
He shall rule the world with justice
   and the peoples with his constancy.

R̸. Today is born our Savior, Christ the Lord.

*See Appendix, p. 200, for Second Reading*

### Reflecting on Living the Gospel

Christmas celebrates more than the birth of a baby; it is a feast of salvation announcing to us that the glory of the Lord is upon us. Christmas calls us to open ourselves to God's glory so that it may shine through us for others.

### Connecting the Responsorial Psalm to the Readings

To us human beings who dwell in darkness, burdened and bloodied, the Savior comes (first reading). He comes not in awe and majesty, but born in the night and laid in a manger (gospel). He comes bringing peace, judgment, and justice. He comes to cleanse us so that we are "eager to do what is good" (second reading). The readings for the Mass at Midnight tell us that Christ takes us as we are and enables us to become much more. And so on this most holy night we join the heavens, the seas, even the trees of the forests in rejoicing, for our Savior has been born, and nothing is the same!

### Psalmist Preparation

As you prepare to sing this responsorial psalm, use the refrain for daily personal prayer. Let joy and gratitude for the gift of the incarnation fill your heart so that what is in your heart may flow out of your voice when you sing this psalm during the liturgy.

### Prayer

God of salvation, you sent your Son to show us light in darkness, hope in hardship, and majesty in littleness. As he took on our humanity, raise us to take on his divinity. We ask this in his name. Amen.

# THE NATIVITY OF THE LORD
## Mass at Dawn

### Gospel (Luke 2:15-20; L15ABC)

When the angels went away from them to heaven, the shepherds said to one another, "Let us go, then, to Bethlehem to see this thing that has taken place, which the Lord has made known to us." So they went in haste and found Mary and Joseph, and the infant lying in the manger. When they saw this, they made known the message that had been told them about this child. All who heard it were amazed by what had been told them by the shepherds. And Mary kept all these things, reflecting on them in her heart. Then the shepherds returned, glorifying and praising God for all they had heard and seen, just as it had been told to them.

### First Reading (Isa 62:11-12)

See, the LORD proclaims
   to the ends of the earth:
say to daughter Zion,
   your savior comes!
Here is his reward with him,
   his recompense before him.
They shall be called the holy people,
   the redeemed of the LORD,
and you shall be called "Frequented,"
   a city that is not forsaken.

### Responsorial Psalm (Ps 97:1, 6, 11-12)

R̘. A light will shine on us this day: the Lord is born for us.

The LORD is king; let the earth rejoice;
   let the many isles be glad.
The heavens proclaim his justice,
   and all peoples see his glory.

R̘. A light will shine on us this day: the Lord is born for us.

Light dawns for the just;
   and gladness, for the upright of heart.

Be glad in the LORD, you just,
  and give thanks to his holy name.

R̸. A light will shine on us this day: the Lord is born for us.

*See Appendix, p. 200, for Second Reading*

### Reflecting on Living the Gospel

We cannot know or recognize the mystery of salvation by ourselves. God alone makes this mystery known to us. Whether God communicates the message through angels or shepherds or others or even ourselves, the message always begs heartfelt reflection and committed response.

### Connecting the Responsorial Psalm to the Readings

Psalm 97 is one of a set of songs (Pss 93; 95–100) celebrating God's kingship over other gods, the forces of nature, and the movements of history. For the cultures of the ancient Near East a god was powerful because of some concrete mighty act. In Psalm 97 God manifests the divine Self in clouds, fire, and lightning, making the earth tremble and mountains melt. While those who worship other gods bend in shame, Israel rejoices and sings God's praises.

The few lines from Psalm 97 chosen for the Mass at Dawn fit the calm and quiet of early morning. The angels singing the midnight theophany of God's glory have dispersed. Now we and the simple shepherds tiptoe to the stable to see what we have been told about, the mighty act of God "lying in a manger" (gospel), "born for us" (psalm refrain) in human flesh.

### Psalmist Preparation

What "light" dawns today? For whom? How does your singing this morning participate in this light?

### Prayer

God of salvation, today your light dawns upon us in the face of your Son come to us in human flesh. May we, like the simple shepherds, tell about this Child to all the world. We ask this in his name. Amen.

**Gospel (John 1:1-18 [or John 1:1-5, 9-14]; L16ABC)**

[In the beginning was the Word,
   and the Word was with God,
   and the Word was God.
He was in the beginning with God.
All things came to be through him,
   and without him nothing came to
      be.
What came to be through him
      was life,
   and this life was the light of the
      human race;
the light shines in the darkness,
   and the darkness has not overcome it.]

A man named John was sent from God. He came for testimony, to testify to the light, so that all might believe through him. He was not the light, but came to testify to the light. [The true light, which enlightens everyone, was coming into the world.

He was in the world,
   and the world came to be through him,
   but the world did not know him.
He came to what was his own,
   but his own people did not accept him.

But to those who did accept him he gave power to become children of God, to those who believe in his name, who were born not by natural generation nor by human choice nor by a man's decision but of God.

And the Word became flesh
   and made his dwelling among us,
   and we saw his glory,
   the glory as of the Father's only Son,
   full of grace and truth.]

John testified to him and cried out, saying, "This was he of whom I said, 'The one who is coming after me ranks ahead of me because he existed before me.'" From his fullness we have all received, grace in place of grace, because while the law was given through Moses, grace and truth came through Jesus Christ. No one has ever seen God. The only Son, God, who is at the Father's side, has revealed him.

### First Reading (Isa 52:7-10)

How beautiful upon the mountains
  are the feet of him who brings glad tidings,
announcing peace, bearing good news,
  announcing salvation, and saying to Zion,
  "Your God is King!"

Hark! Your sentinels raise a cry,
  together they shout for joy,
for they see directly, before their eyes,
  the Lord restoring Zion.
Break out together in song,
  O ruins of Jerusalem!
For the Lord comforts his people,
  he redeems Jerusalem.
The Lord has bared his holy arm
  in the sight of all the nations;
all the ends of the earth will behold
  the salvation of our God.

### Responsorial Psalm (Ps 98:1, 2-3, 3-4, 5-6)

R̘. (3c) All the ends of the earth have seen the saving power of God.

Sing to the Lord a new song,
  for he has done wondrous deeds;
his right hand has won victory for him,
  his holy arm.

R̘. All the ends of the earth have seen the saving power of God.

The Lord has made his salvation known:
  in the sight of the nations he has revealed his justice.
He has remembered his kindness and his faithfulness
  toward the house of Israel.

R̘. All the ends of the earth have seen the saving power of God.

All the ends of the earth have seen
  the salvation by our God.
Sing joyfully to the Lord, all you lands;
  break into song; sing praise.

R̘. All the ends of the earth have seen the saving power of God.

33

Sing praise to the LORD with the harp,
  with the harp and melodious song.
With trumpets and the sound of the horn
  sing joyfully before the King, the LORD.

R̥. All the ends of the earth have seen the saving power of God.

*See Appendix, p. 201, for Second Reading*

### Reflecting on Living the Gospel
In the beginning, God granted existence to all things by speaking a mighty word. God's desire was that we have life. To this end, God's Word assumed human flesh so that "all the ends of the earth will behold the salvation of our God" (first reading). Because of Christ's birth we have received salvation—the very fullness of God, the very fullness of existence.

### Connecting the Responsorial Psalm to the Readings
Psalm 98 is an enthronement psalm celebrating God's sovereignty over all creation and all nations. It uses three typical images—God as king, God as warrior, and God as wielder of power—which can be unsettling if we interpret them only on the literal level of Israel's victory in battle over a political enemy. But when we look deeper into the imagery—and into the core of Israel's faith—we discover a God working tirelessly to transform the order of the world so that the lowly may be uplifted and the righteous blessed. This is a God exercising power to corral the wicked, destroy evil, erase suffering and end oppression. Such is the good news we bear (first reading). But there is more. The gospel announces that through Christ we share in this transforming power. The whole world can sing about the saving power of God because it sees that power working in and through us.

### Psalmist Preparation
You call the assembly not only to sing about the saving power of God revealed in the birth of Jesus but to show that power to the world by the manner in which they live. How might you grow in your own confidence in this power of God within you?

### Prayer
God of salvation, you sent your Word Jesus to dwell among us so that through him we might become your children. Lead us always to live as your daughters and sons who speak only your Word and spread only your Light. We ask this in his name. Amen.

### Gospel (Luke 2:22-40 [or Luke 2:22, 39-40]; L17B)

[When the days were completed for their purification according to the law of Moses, they took him up to Jerusalem to present him to the Lord,] just as it is written in the law of the Lord, *Every male that opens the womb shall be consecrated to the Lord,* and to offer the sacrifice of *a pair of turtledoves or two young pigeons,* in accordance with the dictate in the law of the Lord.

Now there was a man in Jerusalem whose name was Simeon. This man was righteous and devout, awaiting the consolation of Israel, and the Holy Spirit was upon him. It had been revealed to him by the Holy Spirit that he should not see death before he had seen the Christ of the Lord. He came in the Spirit into the temple; and when the parents brought in the child Jesus to perform the custom of the law in regard to him, he took him into his arms and blessed God, saying:

"Now, Master, you may let your servant go
    in peace, according to your word,
for my eyes have seen your salvation,
    which you prepared in sight of all the peoples,
a light for revelation to the Gentiles,
    and glory for your people Israel."

The child's father and mother were amazed at what was said about him; and Simeon blessed them and said to Mary his mother, "Behold, this child is destined for the fall and rise of many in Israel, and to be a sign that will be contradicted—and you yourself a sword will pierce—so that the thoughts of many hearts may be revealed." There was also a prophetess, Anna, the daughter of Phanuel, of the tribe of Asher. She was advanced in years, having lived seven years with her husband after her marriage, and then as a widow until she was eighty-four. She never left the temple, but worshiped night and day with fasting and prayer. And coming forward at that very time, she gave thanks to God and spoke about the child to all who were awaiting the redemption of Jerusalem.

# THE HOLY FAMILY OF JESUS, MARY, AND JOSEPH

[When they had fulfilled all the prescriptions of the law of the Lord, they returned to Galilee, to their own town of Nazareth. The child grew and became strong, filled with wisdom; and the favor of God was upon him.]

### First Reading (Gen 15:1-6, 21:1-3)

The word of the LORD came to Abram in a vision, saying:
"Fear not, Abram!
I am your shield;
I will make your reward very great."
But Abram said,
"O Lord GOD, what good will your gifts be,
if I keep on being childless
and have as my heir the steward of my house, Eliezer?"
Abram continued,
"See, you have given me no offspring,
and so one of my servants will be my heir."
Then the word of the LORD came to him:
"No, that one shall not be your heir;
your own issue shall be your heir."
The Lord took Abram outside and said,
"Look up at the sky and count the stars, if you can.
Just so," he added, "shall your descendants be."
Abram put his faith in the LORD,
who credited it to him as an act of righteousness.

The LORD took note of Sarah as he had said he would;
he did for her as he had promised.
Sarah became pregnant and bore Abraham a son in his old age,
at the set time that God had stated.
Abraham gave the name Isaac to this son of his
whom Sarah bore him.

### or First Reading (Sir 3:2-6, 12-14)

*Responsorial Psalm* (Ps 105:1-2, 3-4, 6-7, 8-9)

R℣. (7a, 8a) The Lord remembers his covenant forever.

Give thanks to the LORD, invoke his name;
   make known among the nations his deeds.
Sing to him, sing his praise,
   proclaim all his wondrous deeds.

R℣. The Lord remembers his covenant forever.

Glory in his holy name;
   rejoice, O hearts that seek the LORD!
Look to the LORD in his strength;
   constantly seek his face.

R℣. The Lord remembers his covenant forever.

You descendants of Abraham, his servants,
   sons of Jacob, his chosen ones!
He, the LORD, is our God;
   throughout the earth his judgments prevail.

R℣. The Lord remembers his covenant forever.

He remembers forever his covenant
   which he made binding for a thousand generations
which he entered into with Abraham
   and by his oath to Isaac.

R℣. The Lord remembers his covenant forever.

*See Appendix, p. 201, for Second Reading*

### Reflecting on Living the Gospel

Mary and Joseph bring Jesus to the temple "according to the *law*," fulfilling their obligation as new parents. Simeon is open to the *Holy Spirit's* Presence, guidance, and revelation to him of the "Christ of the Lord." Anna *spoke prophetically* to others about the redemption that was at hand. Faithfulness to the law, openness to the Holy Spirit, prophetically speaking about what has been revealed deepen our right relationship with God. Families are holy when they, too, act ßas did Mary and Joseph, Simeon, and Anna.

### Connecting the Responsorial Psalm to the Readings

These verses from Psalm 105 relate directly to the story told in the first reading. God promises Abraham offspring when it is no longer possible for Sarah to bear children (second reading). Even more, God promises Abraham and Sarah their offspring will outnumber the stars. Their ultimate progeny would be the Child of Mary and Joseph, the "light of revelation" and gift of salvation to all nations (gospel). For God achieves what human beings cannot, and does so not just for a time, but for all time, not just for one line of descendants, but for all the human family. Indeed, the "Lord remembers his covenant forever" (psalm refrain) with those who are faithful (second reading). For this we, God's holy family, give God thanks.

### Psalmist Preparation

As you prepare to proclaim this psalm spend some time reflecting on the God about whom you will be singing. Who is this God who desires to be in covenant with us? Who is this God who remembers us forever? Who is this God who keeps acting in our favor? And who are we because of this God?

### Prayer

God, you are a Trinity of Persons who has created us to live in loving relationship with one another. Keep us faithful to our covenant relationship with you and with each other that we may be blessed and favored in your sight. We ask this through Christ our Lord. Amen.

### Gospel (Luke 2:16-21; L18ABC)

The shepherds went in haste to Bethlehem and found Mary and Joseph, and the infant lying in the manger. When they saw this, they made known the message that had been told them about this child. All who heard it were amazed by what had been told them by the shepherds. And Mary kept all these things, reflecting on them in her heart. Then the shepherds returned, glorifying and praising God for all they had heard and seen, just as it had been told to them.

When eight days were completed for his circumcision, he was named Jesus, the name given him by the angel before he was conceived in the womb.

### First Reading (Num 6:22-27)

The Lord said to Moses: "Speak to Aaron and his sons and tell them: This is how you shall bless the Israelites. Say to them:

The Lord bless you and keep you!
The Lord let his face shine upon you, and be gracious to you!
The Lord look upon you kindly and give you peace!

So shall they invoke my name upon the Israelites, and I will bless them."

### Responsorial Psalm (Ps 67:2-3, 5, 6, 8)

R̸. (2a) May God bless us in his mercy.

May God have pity on us and bless us;
    may he let his face shine upon us.
So may your way be known upon earth;
    among all nations, your salvation.

R̸. May God bless us in his mercy.

May the nations be glad and exult
    because you rule the peoples in equity;
    the nations on the earth you guide.

R̸. May God bless us in his mercy.

May the peoples praise you, O God;
> may all the peoples praise you!

May God bless us,
> and may all the ends of the earth fear him!

R7. May God bless us in his mercy.

*See Appendix, p. 201, for Second Reading*

### Reflecting on Living the Gospel

This infant conceived by the Holy Spirit in Mary's womb is both God and man. No doubt Mary reflected "in her heart" on this great mystery throughout her life, a reflection that preserved her as the holy and faithful Mother of God. Our reflection on the mystery of the incarnation must be so deep as Mary's that it brings us to greater holiness and faithfulness. It must bring us, like the shepherds, to come in haste to encounter the One who deserves all glory and praise.

### Connecting the Responsorial Psalm to the Readings

The Lectionary omits the verse from Psalm 67 which marks it as a song of thanksgiving for a bountiful harvest: "The earth has yielded its harvest; / God, our God, blesses us" (v. 7). In singing Psalm 67 the Israelites not only thanked God for all that had been given to them but also asked God to extend this bounty to all peoples. On this solemnity we celebrate that the mercy of God has caused the earthly flesh of Mary to yield its greatest blessing, the body of Jesus (gospel). And through this blessing we are harvested as God's own children (second reading). In singing Psalm 67 we acknowledge the unimaginable magnitude of God's mercy toward us, and we pray that all peoples come to know their blessedness in Christ.

### Psalmist Preparation

As you prepare to sing Psalm 67, reflect on how blessed you are because of the birth of Christ. Do you know that you are a child of God? Do you know how favored you are? What might you do this week to lead others to discover their blessedness?

### Prayer

Saving God, you brought the mystery of salvation to fulfillment in the flesh of Mary. May we, with her, contemplate this wondrous blessing that brings heaven to earth. We ask this through Christ our Lord. Amen.

### Gospel (Matt 2:1-12; L20ABC)

When Jesus was born in Bethlehem of Judea, in the days of King Herod, behold, magi from the east arrived in Jerusalem, saying, "Where is the newborn king of the Jews? We saw his star at its rising and have come to do him homage." When King Herod heard this, he was greatly troubled, and all Jerusalem with him. Assembling all the chief priests and the scribes of the people, he inquired of them where the Christ was to be born. They said to him, "In Bethlehem of Judea, for thus it has been written through the prophet:

> *And you, Bethlehem, land of Judah,*
> *   are by no means least among the rulers of Judah;*
> *since from you shall come a ruler,*
> *   who is to shepherd my people Israel."*

Then Herod called the magi secretly and ascertained from them the time of the star's appearance. He sent them to Bethlehem and said, "Go and search diligently for the child. When you have found him, bring me word, that I too may go and do him homage." After their audience with the king they set out. And behold, the star that they had seen at its rising preceded them, until it came and stopped over the place where the child was. They were overjoyed at seeing the star, and on entering the house they saw the child with Mary his mother. They prostrated themselves and did him homage. Then they opened their treasures and offered him gifts of gold, frankincense, and myrrh. And having been warned in a dream not to return to Herod, they departed for their country by another way.

### First Reading (Isa 60:1-6)

Rise up in splendor, Jerusalem! Your light has come,
   the glory of the Lord shines upon you.
See, darkness covers the earth,
   and thick clouds cover the peoples;
but upon you the LORD shines,
   and over you appears his glory.
Nations shall walk by your light,
   and kings by your shining radiance.
Raise your eyes and look about;
   they all gather and come to you:
your sons come from afar,
   and your daughters in the arms of
      their nurses.

Then you shall be radiant at what you see,
　　your heart shall throb and overflow,
for the riches of the sea shall be emptied out before you,
　　the wealth of nations shall be brought to you.
Caravans of camels shall fill you,
　　dromedaries from Midian and Ephah;
all from Sheba shall come
　　bearing gold and frankincense,
　　and proclaiming the praises of the LORD.

### Responsorial Psalm (Ps 72:1-2, 7-8, 10-11, 12-13)

R̸. (cf. 11) Lord, every nation on earth will adore you.

O God, with your judgment endow the king,
　　and with your justice, the king's son;
he shall govern your people with justice
　　and your afflicted ones with judgment.

R̸. Lord, every nation on earth will adore you.

Justice shall flower in his days,
　　and profound peace, till the moon be no more.
May he rule from sea to sea,
　　and from the River to the ends of the earth.

R̸. Lord, every nation on earth will adore you.

The kings of Tarshish and the Isles shall offer gifts;
　　the kings of Arabia and Seba shall bring tribute.
All kings shall pay him homage,
　　all nations shall serve him.

R̸. Lord, every nation on earth will adore you.

For he shall rescue the poor when he cries out,
　　and the afflicted when he has no one to help him.
He shall have pity for the lowly and the poor;
　　the lives of the poor he shall save.

R̸. Lord, every nation on earth will adore you.

*See Appendix, p. 202, for Second Reading*

### Reflecting on Living the Gospel

This gospel uncovers a number of contrasts: the magi-Gentiles from the
east vs. Herod and the Jews of all Jerusalem; the light of the star that

guided the magi vs. the darkness of Herod's heart; the "newborn king of the Jews" thought to be found in Jerusalem vs. this Child being found in the small village of Bethlehem; Herod breeding evil in his heart to keep his power and status vs. the magi who paid homage and offered gifts to the Child. Searching for and finding the Christ necessitates a choice in face of contrasts.

### Connecting the Responsorial Psalm to the Readings
Psalm 72 was both a royal psalm used at coronation ceremonies and a messianic text which looked forward to the fullness of God's reign over all nations. For Israel, the king was the arm of God's righteousness among the people. He protected the well-being of the kingdom by seeing that the poor and needy were given justice. The Hebrew word *shalom* ("peace" in verse 7) meant a situation where everyone had whatever was needed to live. The health of the nation, then, was measured by the condition of every member, especially those who were poor, and responsibility for that condition rested with the king.

Christ is the fulfillment of this kingly role. He "rescue[s] the poor" and shows "pity for the lowly." He brings about the full flowering of "justice" and "profound peace." Moreover, his reign is not limited to Israel but encompasses all nations (second reading, gospel). In Christ *shalom* has come for all peoples. The magi went to great lengths to find this King (gospel); may we who have also found this King go to the same lengths to lead every nation into his kingdom of *shalom*.

### Psalmist Preparation
Knowing the background of this responsorial psalm will help you sing it with greater understanding of its relationship to the solemnity of the Epiphany. Much of the psalm is intercessory prayer for the king that he be able to fulfill his mission of implementing God's plan of justice and peace for the poor. This was a tall order; even Christ the King was not able to fill it without the sacrifice of his life.

Through baptism we are God's kingly people. This means that all nations will come to adore Christ if we lead them through lives of justice and peace. Your singing of this psalm is not only proclamation of what will be but also invitation that we, God's kingly people, help make it happen.

### Prayer
Redeeming God, you sent your Son to be salvation for all peoples. Fill us with his light that we may be his redeeming presence to all whom we meet. We ask this in his name. Amen.

### Gospel (Mark 1:7-11; L21B)

This is what John the Baptist proclaimed: "One mightier than I is coming
after me. I am not worthy to stoop and
loosen the thongs of his sandals. I
have baptized you with water; he will
baptize you with the Holy Spirit."

It happened in those days that
Jesus came from Nazareth of Galilee and was baptized in the Jordan
by John. On coming up out of the
water he saw the heavens being torn open and the Spirit, like a dove, de-
scending upon him. And a voice came from the heavens, "You are my beloved Son; with you I am well pleased."

### First Reading (Isa 55:1-11)

Thus says the LORD:
All you who are thirsty,
    come to the water!
You who have no money,
    come, receive grain and eat;
come, without paying and without cost,
    drink wine and milk!
Why spend your money for what is not bread,
    your wages for what fails to satisfy?
Heed me, and you shall eat well,
    you shall delight in rich fare.
Come to me heedfully,
    listen, that you may have life.
I will renew with you the everlasting covenant,
    the benefits assured to David.
As I made him a witness to the peoples,
    a leader and commander of nations,
so shall you summon a nation you knew not,
    and nations that knew you not shall run to you,
because of the LORD, your God,
    the Holy One of Israel, who has glorified you.

Seek the LORD while he may be found,
    call him while he is near.

Let the scoundrel forsake his way,
    and the wicked man his thoughts;
let him turn to the LORD for mercy;
    to our God, who is generous in forgiving.
For my thoughts are not your thoughts,
    nor are your ways my ways, says the LORD.
As high as the heavens are above the earth
    so high are my ways above your ways
    and my thoughts above your thoughts.

For just as from the heavens
    the rain and snow come down
and do not return there
    till they have watered the earth,
    making it fertile and fruitful,
giving seed to the one who sows
    and bread to the one who eats,
so shall my word be
    that goes forth from my mouth;
my word shall not return to me void,
    but shall do my will,
    achieving the end for which I sent it.

**or First Reading (Isa 42:1-4, 6-7)**

**Responsorial Psalm (Isa 12:2-3, 4bcd, 5-6)**

R℣. (3) You will draw water joyfully from the springs of salvation.

God indeed is my savior;
    I am confident and unafraid.
My strength and my courage is the LORD,
    and he has been my savior.
With joy you will draw water
    at the fountain of salvation.

R℣. You will draw water joyfully from the springs of salvation.

Give thanks to the LORD, acclaim his name;
    among the nations make known his deeds,
    proclaim how exalted is his name.

R℣. You will draw water joyfully from the springs of salvation.

Sing praise to the LORD for his glorious achievement;
    let this be known throughout all the earth.

45

Shout with exultation, O city of Zion,
  for great in your midst
  is the Holy One of Israel!

R̶. You will draw water joyfully from the springs of salvation.

**or Responsorial Psalm (Ps 29:1-2, 3-4, 3, 9-10)**

*See Appendix, p. 202, for Second Reading*

### Reflecting on Living the Gospel

Jesus' baptism did not change his identity, but revealed who he was. John prophesied that Jesus, however, would bring an entirely different baptism, for he would baptize us with the Holy Spirit. The event of our baptism with the Spirit announces to all present who we become: beloved children with whom God is also "well pleased." Our whole Christian life is a journey of taking ownership of the ownership God has already taken of us. Through baptism God claims us.

### Connecting the Responsorial Psalm to the Readings

The responsorial psalm this Sunday is not taken from the Psalter but from the book of Isaiah. The verses are part of a song celebrating God's deliverance of Israel from disaster and destruction. The psalmist proclaims God savior and calls all Israel to spread the news of God's saving intervention to "all the earth."

The salvation God offers is the gift of covenant relationship (first and second readings) celebrated with the fullness of the messianic banquet (first reading). It is the gift of personal relationship with God and one another marked by love (second reading). This gift is free but not without its demand that we change our manner of living (first and second readings). We can accept the gift and take on its demand because, through Jesus, we have been baptized with the Holy Spirit who will give us the strength and courage we need (psalm).

### Psalmist Preparation

In this Sunday's responsorial psalm you sing about God's gift of salvation. The readings reveal that salvation means our adoption as God's children, our feasting freely at the messianic meal, and our communion with one another. How have you experienced this salvation? How have you enabled others to share in it?

### Prayer

Omnipotent God, in the waters of baptism you flood us with your grace and goodness. Help us take up our baptismal mission to be this grace and goodness in the world. We ask this through Christ our Lord. Amen.

### Gospel (John 1:35-42; L65B)

John was standing with two of his disciples, and as he watched Jesus walk by, he said, "Behold, the Lamb of God." The two disciples heard what he said and followed Jesus. Jesus turned and saw them following him and said to them, "What are you looking for?" They said to him, "Rabbi"— which translated means Teacher—, "where are you staying?" He said to them, "Come, and you will see." So they went and saw where Jesus was staying, and they stayed with him that day. It was about four in the afternoon. Andrew, the brother of Simon Peter, was one of the two who heard John and followed Jesus. He first found his own brother Simon and told him, "We have found the Messiah"—which is translated Christ. Then he brought him to Jesus. Jesus looked at him and said, "You are Simon the son of John; you will be called Cephas"—which is translated Peter.

### First Reading (1 Sam 3:3b-10, 19)

Samuel was sleeping in the temple of the LORD where the ark of God was. The LORD called to Samuel, who answered, "Here I am." Samuel ran to Eli and said, "Here I am. You called me." "I did not call you," Eli said. "Go back to sleep." So he went back to sleep. Again the LORD called Samuel, who rose and went to Eli. "Here I am," he said. "You called me." But Eli answered, "I did not call you, my son. Go back to sleep."

At that time Samuel was not familiar with the LORD, because the LORD had not revealed anything to him as yet. The LORD called Samuel again, for the third time. Getting up and going to Eli, he said, "Here I am. You called me." Then Eli understood that the LORD was calling the youth. So he said to Samuel, "Go to sleep, and if you are called, reply, 'Speak, LORD, for your servant is listening.'" When Samuel went to sleep in his place, the LORD came and revealed his presence, calling out as before, "Samuel, Samuel!" Samuel answered, "Speak, for your servant is listening."

Samuel grew up, and the LORD was with him, not permitting any word of his to be without effect.

### Responsorial Psalm (Ps 40:2, 4, 7-8, 8-9, 10)

℞. (8a and 9a) Here am I, Lord; I come to do your will.

I have waited, waited for the LORD,
  and he stooped toward me and heard my cry.
And he put a new song into my mouth,
  a hymn to our God.

℞. Here am I, Lord; I come to do your will.

Sacrifice or offering you wished not,
  but ears open to obedience you gave me.
Holocausts or sin-offerings you sought not;
  then said I, "Behold I come."

℞. Here am I, Lord; I come to do your will.

"In the written scroll it is prescribed for me,
to do your will, O my God, is my delight,
  and your law is within my heart!"

℞. Here am I, Lord; I come to do your will.

I announced your justice in the vast assembly;
  I did not restrain my lips, as you, O LORD, know.

℞. Here am I, Lord; I come to do your will.

### Reflecting on Living the Gospel
The two disciples in the gospel would have interpreted John the Baptist's cry, "Behold, the Lamb of God," within the Passover and temple tradition of sacrifice of lambs. What is startling about John's cry is that he uses this sacrificial reference not for a lamb, an animal, but for a human being who was walking by—Jesus. John is pointing to Jesus as the One who will be sacrificed. Little did they know at this point that the core of following Jesus is sacrifice—a total self-giving. Still, they followed him.

### Connecting the Responsorial Psalm to the Readings
In Psalm 40, the one praying offers God thanksgiving for having been rescued from life-threatening danger. Having waited for God's help and not been disappointed, the person bursts into a "new song," praising God before all the world. But the psalmist also realizes it is not enough to offer God an external sacrifice of thanksgiving. What God seeks is the lifelong, all-consuming offering of a human heart willing to do God's will.

In these verses from Psalm 40 we express our willingness to do God's will with all our hearts. We choose, like Samuel, to keep listening until we recognize God's voice. We choose, like the disciples, to come close to Jesus so that we may know him better and follow him more fully. We choose, like Jesus the Lamb of God, to give our very selves so that others may have life. This choice will change our lives. Is this not what the journey of Ordinary Time is about?

### Psalmist Preparation

As you prepare to sing this Sunday's responsorial psalm spend some time reflecting on why this psalm and these readings were selected for the Second Sunday in Ordinary Time. What is Ordinary Time calling you to do? to become? What are you as psalmist calling the assembly to do? to become?

### Prayer

God of redemption, you call us to follow your Son Jesus in a life of obedience to your will. Grant us the courage to say yes and the grace to remain faithful. We ask this in his name. Amen.

### Gospel (Mark 1:14-20; L68B)

After John had been arrested, Jesus came to Galilee proclaiming the gospel of God: "This is the time of fulfillment. The kingdom of God is at hand. Repent, and believe in the gospel."

As he passed by the Sea of Galilee, he saw Simon and his brother Andrew casting their nets into the sea; they were fishermen. Jesus said to them, "Come after me, and I will make you fishers of men." Then they abandoned their nets and followed him. He walked along a little farther and saw James, the son of Zebedee, and his brother John. They too were in a boat mending their nets. Then he called them. So they left their father Zebedee in the boat along with the hired men and followed him.

### First Reading (Jonah 3:1-5, 10)

The word of the LORD came to Jonah, saying: "Set out for the great city of Nineveh, and announce to it the message that I will tell you." So Jonah made ready and went to Nineveh, according to the LORD's bidding. Now Nineveh was an enormously large city; it took three days to go through it. Jonah began his journey through the city, and had gone but a single day's walk announcing, "Forty days more and Nineveh shall be destroyed," when the people of Nineveh believed God; they proclaimed a fast and all of them, great and small, put on sackcloth.

When God saw by their actions how they turned from their evil way, he repented of the evil that he had threatened to do to them; he did not carry it out.

### Responsorial Psalm (Ps 25:4-5, 6-7, 8-9)

R̝. (4a) Teach me your ways, O Lord.

Your ways, O LORD, make known to me;
    teach me your paths,
Guide me in your truth and teach me,
    for you are God my savior.

R̝. Teach me your ways, O Lord.

Remember that your compassion, O LORD,
    and your love are from of old.
In your kindness remember me,
    because of your goodness, O LORD.

R̝. Teach me your ways, O Lord.

Good and upright is the LORD;
    thus he shows sinners the way.

He guides the humble to justice
　　and teaches the humble his way.

R̸. Teach me your ways, O Lord.

### Reflecting on Living the Gospel

John preached repentance, and was arrested in spite of his goodness and innocence. Jesus preached the Gospel and suffered and died in spite of his goodness and innocence. Hearing Jesus' call to discipleship and choosing to follow him faithfully literally assures us we will meet adversity and suffering, as did both John and Jesus. The surprise of the gospel is not that we will face adversity, however. The surprise is that in preaching repentance and changing our lives, "the time of fulfillment" is upon us. To enter into this "time of fulfillment," we must leave everything behind and answer Jesus' call to follow him.

### Connecting the Responsorial Psalm to the Readings

The Ninevites listen to Jonah's call to repentance and immediately reform their lives (first reading). The disciples hear Jesus' announcement of the kingdom of God and instantly abandon all to follow him (gospel). In Psalm 25 we pray for this same readiness to hear and to learn the ways of God. We acknowledge that the kingdom of God is at hand and ask for the grace to change our lives accordingly. Psalm 25, then, is a blueprint for our journey through Ordinary Time when God teaches and we learn the way of discipleship. May we sing it with confidence, courage, and commitment.

### Psalmist Preparation

As you sing these verses from Psalm 25 you become an icon before the assembly of response to God's call to conversion and discipleship. To help you prepare for this role, spend some time this week reflecting on these questions: Where in your life right now is God calling you to conversion? Through whom is God calling you? What does God wish to teach you?

### Prayer

God of salvation, now is the time of fulfillment when you call us to leave all for the sake of your kingdom. Grant us the courage we need to choose whatever life changes your call will demand of us. We ask this through Christ our Lord. Amen.

### *Gospel* (Mark 1:21-28; L71B)

Then they came to Capernaum, and on the sabbath Jesus entered the synagogue and taught. The people were astonished at his teaching, for he taught them as one having authority and not as the scribes. In their synagogue was a man with an unclean spirit; he cried out, "What have you to do with us, Jesus of Nazareth? Have you come to destroy us? I know who you are—the Holy One of God!" Jesus rebuked him and said, "Quiet! Come out of him!" The unclean spirit convulsed him and with a loud cry came out of him. All were amazed and asked one another, "What is this? A new teaching with authority. He commands even the unclean spirits and they obey him." His fame spread everywhere throughout the whole region of Galilee.

### *First Reading* (Deut 18:15-20)

Moses spoke to all the people, saying: "A prophet like me will the LORD, your God, raise up for you from among your own kin; to him you shall listen. This is exactly what you requested of the LORD, your God, at Horeb on the day of the assembly, when you said, 'Let us not again hear the voice of the LORD, our God, nor see this great fire any more, lest we die.' And the LORD said to me, 'This was well said. I will raise up for them a prophet like you from among their kin, and will put my words into his mouth; he shall tell them all that I command him. Whoever will not listen to my words which he speaks in my name, I myself will make him answer for it. But if a prophet presumes to speak in my name an oracle that I have not commanded him to speak, or speaks in the name of other gods, he shall die.'"

### *Responsorial Psalm* (Ps 95:1-2, 6-7, 7-9)

R℟. (8) If today you hear his voice, harden not your hearts.

Come, let us sing joyfully to the LORD;
    let us acclaim the rock of our salvation.
Let us come into his presence with thanksgiving;
    let us joyfully sing psalms to him.

R℟. If today you hear his voice, harden not your hearts.

Come, let us bow down in worship;
  let us kneel before the Lord who made us.
For he is our God,
  and we are the people he shepherds, the flock he guides.

R̄. If today you hear his voice, harden not your hearts.

Oh, that today you would hear his voice:
  "Harden not your hearts as at Meribah,
  as in the day of Massah in the desert,
Where your fathers tempted me;
  they tested me though they had seen my works."

R̄. If today you hear his voice, harden not your hearts.

### Reflecting on Living the Gospel

All of us must confront many battles waged between good and evil throughout our lives. For us to destroy the evil that confronts us, we must be "of God," we must be holy. We have the authority to banish evil because, baptized into Christ, we are holy ones "of God." The authority of holiness is our baptismal birthright. It is God's Life given us that makes us holy; it is God's Life that makes us, too, "of God." Like Jesus, we must be the authority of holiness incarnate.

### Connecting the Responsorial Psalm to the Readings

These verses from Psalm 95 challenge us to hear the voice of God. In the first reading Moses and the prophets speak the words of God and do so in the recognizable voice of a fellow human being, a "kinsman." In the gospel, Jesus does the same—speaks the word of God in a human voice. But he does so with an authority far beyond anything the people have heard before. The words he speaks are a direct and victorious confrontation with the forces of evil which can possess the human heart.

But the psalm raises the question each of us faces in our struggle with faithful discipleship: will we surrender to this authority? The truth is that, despite how good the news Christ speaks, many elements in our hearts resist. The psalmist pleads with us to remain faithful in our listening to God, knowing full well how real is the possibility that we may choose otherwise. This psalm is a reality check; may we heed its message.

**Psalmist Preparation**

Your singing of this psalm needs to come from a heart that hears the voice of God and responds. Just as God called the Israelites to be holy and faithful, so does God call you. What helps you hear and heed God's voice? What hinders you?

**Prayer**

God of power and might, you sent your Son among us with the voice of authority over illness and evil. May we listen always to his voice and rejoice always in his mighty works of redemption. We ask this in his name. Amen.

### Gospel (Mark 1:29-39; L74B)

On leaving the synagogue Jesus entered the house of Simon and Andrew with James and John. Simon's mother-in-law lay sick with a fever. They immediately told him about her. He approached, grasped her hand, and helped her up. Then the fever left her and she waited on them.

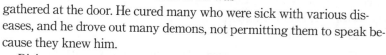

When it was evening, after sunset, they brought to him all who were ill or possessed by demons. The whole town was gathered at the door. He cured many who were sick with various diseases, and he drove out many demons, not permitting them to speak because they knew him.

Rising very early before dawn, he left and went off to a deserted place, where he prayed. Simon and those who were with him pursued him and on finding him said, "Everyone is looking for you." He told them, "Let us go on to the nearby villages that I may preach there also. For this purpose have I come." So he went into their synagogues, preaching and driving out demons throughout the whole of Galilee.

### First Reading (Job 7:1-4, 6-7)

Job spoke, saying:

> Is not man's life on earth a drudgery?
> > Are not his days those of hirelings?
> He is a slave who longs for the shade,
> > a hireling who waits for his wages.
> So I have been assigned months of misery,
> > and troubled nights have been allotted to me.
> If in bed I say, "When shall I arise?"
> > then the night drags on;
> > I am filled with restlessness until the dawn.
> My days are swifter than a weaver's shuttle;
> > they come to an end without hope.
> Remember that my life is like the wind;
> > I shall not see happiness again.

### Responsorial Psalm (Ps 147:1-2, 3-4, 5-6)

R⁊. (cf. 3a) Praise the Lord, who heals the brokenhearted.
*or:* R⁊. Alleluia.

Praise the Lᴏʀᴅ, for he is good;
    sing praise to our God, for he is gracious;
    it is fitting to praise him.
The Lᴏʀᴅ rebuilds Jerusalem;
    the dispersed of Israel he gathers.

R⁊. Praise the Lord, who heals the brokenhearted. *or:* R⁊. Alleluia.

He heals the brokenhearted
    and binds up their wounds.
He tells the number of the stars;
    he calls each by name.

R⁊. Praise the Lord, who heals the brokenhearted. *or:* R⁊. Alleluia.

Great is our Lord and mighty in power;
    to his wisdom there is no limit.
The Lᴏʀᴅ sustains the lowly;
    the wicked he casts to the ground.

R⁊. Praise the Lord, who heals the brokenhearted. *or:* R⁊. Alleluia.

### Reflecting on Living the Gospel

In the gospel Simon says to Jesus, "Everyone is looking for you." Jesus is having great success healing many people and driving out demons. All who encounter him adore him. People are paying great attention to him—"The whole town was gathered" at the door of Simon and Andrew's house. Nonetheless, Jesus moves on to other villages. His ministry is not about drawing attention to himself, but about preaching the Good News of salvation. Yet his ministry *is* about himself, for he *is* the Good News.

### Connecting the Responsorial Psalm to the Readings

The first reading from Job painfully depicts the "drudgery," "restlessness," and "troubled nights" of the human condition. We hear these lines aware of the rest of Job's story: the destruction of his family, the loss of his property, his prolonged and painful illnesses, his degradation by friends and neighbors—all allowed by a God who seemed not to care. By contrast, the gospel reading reveals the truth about God's response to our condition: in the person of Jesus, God comes into human history preaching the Good News of salvation, healing illness, and driving out evil. This is clearly a God who does care.

In the responsorial psalm we proclaim that God heals the broken-hearted, binds the wounded, and sustains the lowly. We tell the world that into the midst of human suffering God comes with power and changes how things are. We become the Good News of salvation.

### Psalmist Preparation

How this week might you bring the Good News of salvation to someone who is brokenhearted, or discouraged, or restless, or without hope?

### Prayer

Saving God, you sent your Son into the world to heal our brokenness and banish our despair. May we sing your praise as we grasp in joy the hand he reaches out to us in mercy. We ask this through him, our Brother and Savior. Amen.

### Gospel (Mark 1:40-45; L77B)

A leper came to Jesus and kneeling down begged him and said, "If you wish, you can make me clean." Moved with pity, he stretched out his hand, touched him, and said to him, "I do will it. Be made clean." The leprosy left him immediately, and he was made clean. Then, warning him sternly, he dismissed him at once.

He said to him, "See that you tell no one anything, but go, show yourself to the priest and offer for your cleansing what Moses prescribed; that will be proof for them."

The man went away and began to publicize the whole matter. He spread the report abroad so that it was impossible for Jesus to enter a town openly. He remained outside in deserted places, and people kept coming to him from everywhere.

### First Reading (Lev 13:1-2, 44-46)

The LORD said to Moses and Aaron, "If someone has on his skin a scab or pustule or blotch which appears to be the sore of leprosy, he shall be brought to Aaron, the priest, or to one of the priests among his descendants. If the man is leprous and unclean, the priest shall declare him unclean by reason of the sore on his head.

"The one who bears the sore of leprosy shall keep his garments rent and his head bare, and shall muffle his beard; he shall cry out, 'Unclean, unclean!' As long as the sore is on him he shall declare himself unclean, since he is in fact unclean. He shall dwell apart, making his abode outside the camp."

### Responsorial Psalm (Ps 32:1-2, 5, 11)

R̰. (7) I turn to you, Lord, in time of trouble, and you fill me with the joy of salvation.

Blessed is he whose fault is taken away,
　　whose sin is covered.
Blessed the man to whom the LORD imputes not guilt,
　　in whose spirit there is no guile.

℟. I turn to you, Lord, in time of trouble, and you fill me with the joy of salvation.

Then I acknowledged my sin to you,
>    my guilt I covered not.
I said, "I confess my faults to the LORD,"
>    and you took away the guilt of my sin.

℟. I turn to you, Lord, in time of trouble, and you fill me with the joy of salvation.

Be glad in the LORD and rejoice, you just;
>    exult, all you upright of heart.

℟. I turn to you, Lord, in time of trouble, and you fill me with the joy of salvation.

### Reflecting on Living the Gospel

This healing account between a leper and Jesus dramatically unfolds in a conversation punctuated by concrete and very personal gestures. The leper comes to Jesus, kneels, and boldly begs for cleansing, gestures expressing his sense of unworthiness. Moved with pity, Jesus stretches out his hand and touches the leper, gestures revealing the leper's inherent dignity. Freed from pain and isolation, the leper can let his inherent dignity spill over into proclaiming the Good News of a new Presence, a new Awakening, a new Life.

### Connecting the Responsorial Psalm to the Readings

Because the readings this Sunday move so quickly from the Old Testament notion of the uncleanness of leprosy to the responsorial psalm's confession of sin and guilt, we can be misled into thinking that serious illness and serious sin are interrelated. The point of the readings and psalm, however, is quite different. What ties the first reading, gospel, and psalm together is our willingness to admit our condition before God, be it ostracizing disease or sinful behavior, and God's readiness to heal and to forgive us. God will counter whatever debilities illness or sin create. We need but ask. May we, like this psalmist and this leper, turn to God with our "trouble" (psalm). And may we then tell everyone what happened when we did.

### Psalmist Preparation

To prepare to sing this psalm, reflect on a time when you experienced alienation from God and others. What caused this rift? Who or what helped you turn to God for healing? What did you learn from this experience about the mercy of God? How can you tell this story in your singing of this psalm?

### Prayer

Healing God, when we are in trouble or pain, you act to save us. Break down whatever barriers keep us from turning to you and lead us to the joy of your salvation. We ask this through Christ our Lord. Amen.

### Gospel (Matt 6:1-6, 16-18; L219)

Jesus said to his disciples: "Take care not to perform righteous deeds in order that people may see them; otherwise, you will have no recompense from your heavenly Father. When you give alms, do not blow a trumpet before you, as the hypocrites do in the synagogues and in the streets to win the praise of others. Amen, I say to you, they have received their reward. But when you give alms, do not let your left hand know what your right is doing, so that your almsgiving may be secret. And your Father who sees in secret will repay you.

"When you pray, do not be like the hypocrites, who love to stand and pray in the synagogues and on street corners so that others may see them. Amen, I say to you, they have received their reward. But when you pray, go to your inner room, close the door, and pray to your Father in secret. And your Father who sees in secret will repay you.

"When you fast, do not look gloomy like the hypocrites. They neglect their appearance, so that they may appear to others to be fasting. Amen, I say to you, they have received their reward. But when you fast, anoint your head and wash your face, so that you may not appear to be fasting, except to your Father who is hidden. And your Father who sees what is hidden will repay you."

### First Reading (Joel 2:12-18)

Even now, says the LORD,
>   return to me with your whole heart,
>   with fasting, and weeping, and mourning;
Rend your hearts, not your garments,
>   and return to the LORD, your God.
For gracious and merciful is he,
>   slow to anger, rich in kindness,
>   and relenting in punishment.
Perhaps he will again relent
>   and leave behind him a blessing,
Offerings and libations
>   for the LORD, your God.

Blow the trumpet in Zion!
    proclaim a fast,
    call an assembly;
Gather the people,
    notify the congregation;
Assemble the elders,
    gather the children
    and the infants at the breast;
Let the bridegroom quit his room,
    and the bride her chamber.
Between the porch and the altar
    let the priests, the ministers of the LORD, weep,
And say, "Spare, O LORD, your people,
    and make not your heritage a reproach,
    with the nations ruling over them!
Why should they say among the peoples,
    'Where is their God?'"

Then the LORD was stirred to concern for his land
    and took pity on his people.

### Responsorial Psalm (Ps 51:3-4, 5-6ab, 12-13, 14 and 17)

R̸. (see 3a) Be merciful, O Lord, for we have sinned.

Have mercy on me, O God, in your goodness;
    in the greatness of your compassion wipe out my offense.
Thoroughly wash me from my guilt
    and of my sin cleanse me.

R̸. Be merciful, O Lord, for we have sinned.

For I acknowledge my offense,
    and my sin is before me always:
"Against you only have I sinned,
    and done what is evil in your sight."

R̸. Be merciful, O Lord, for we have sinned.

A clean heart create for me, O God,
    and a steadfast spirit renew within me.
Cast me not out from your presence,
    and your Holy Spirit take not from me.

R̸. Be merciful, O Lord, for we have sinned.

Give me back the joy of your salvation,
   and a willing spirit sustain in me.
O Lord, open my lips,
   and my mouth shall proclaim your praise.

R⃒. Be merciful, O Lord, for we have sinned.

*See Appendix, p. 202, for Second Reading*

### Reflecting on Living the Gospel

Three times in this gospel Jesus tells us to do "righteous deeds" not to be noticed by others, but to be repaid by God. This repayment is nothing less than the righteousness of a deepened relationship with God. Our "righteous deeds"—our Lenten penances—are to be directed to forming a new habit of righteous relationship. Ironically, what we have done "in secret" *will* be noticed by others—not for the deeds themselves, but for who, through these deeds, we become.

### Connecting the Responsorial Psalm to the Readings

As we do every year, we begin our annual season of penance and transformation by singing Psalm 51. Of all the penitential psalms, Psalm 51 is the most open in its confession of sin and the most poignant in its plea for God's mercy. Psalm 51 takes us to that "secret" place (gospel) where we "rend our hearts" (first reading) so that God may change them (psalm). The good news is that God will do the cleansing work of transforming our inner selves (psalm). We have only to open our hearts and ask.

### Psalmist Preparation

In singing Psalm 51 you acknowledge that you have not always been faithful and ask God to bring you back by re-creating your heart. You stand before the assembly as a living embodiment of both sides of the story of salvation: human sinfulness and divine mercy. Such witness demands a great deal of honesty and vulnerability. What can help you be honest before God? What can help you be vulnerable before the community?

### Prayer

God of compassion, you embrace in mercy the sinner who returns to you with a contrite heart. Lead us through our Lenten practices of prayer, penance, and almsgiving to turn our hearts more fully toward you that we may rise transformed with new life on Easter. We ask this through Christ our Lord. Amen.

### Gospel (Mark 1:12-15; L23B)

The Spirit drove Jesus out into the desert, and he remained in the desert for forty days, tempted by Satan. He was among wild beasts, and the angels ministered to him.

After John had been arrested, Jesus came to Galilee proclaiming the gospel of God: "This is the time of fulfillment. The kingdom of God is at hand. Repent, and believe in the gospel."

### First Reading (Gen 9:8-15)

God said to Noah and to his sons with him: "See, I am now establishing my covenant with you and your descendants after you and with every living creature that was with you: all the birds, and the various tame and wild animals that were with you and came out of the ark. I will establish my covenant with you, that never again shall all bodily creatures be destroyed by the waters of a flood; there shall not be another flood to devastate the earth." God added: "This is the sign that I am giving for all ages to come, of the covenant between me and you and every living creature with you: I set my bow in the clouds to serve as a sign of the covenant between me and the earth. When I bring clouds over the earth, and the bow appears in the clouds, I will recall the covenant I have made between me and you and all living beings, so that the waters shall never again become a flood to destroy all mortal beings."

### Responsorial Psalm (Ps 25:4-5, 6-7, 8-9)

R℣. (cf. 10) Your ways, O Lord, are love and truth to those who keep your covenant.

Your ways, O Lord, make known to me;
　　teach me your paths,
Guide me in your truth and teach me,
　　for you are God my savior.

R℣. Your ways, O Lord, are love and truth to those who keep your covenant.

Remember that your compassion, O Lord,
　　and your love are from of old.
In your kindness remember me,
　　because of your goodness, O Lord.

R℣. Your ways, O Lord, are love and truth to those who keep your covenant.

Good and upright is the LORD,
    thus he shows sinners the way.
He guides the humble to justice,
    and he teaches the humble his way.

R℣. Your ways, O Lord, are love and truth to those who keep your covenant.

*See Appendix, p. 202, for Second Reading*

### Reflecting on Living the Gospel

Mark does not relay the details of Jesus' experience of temptation, but he does show its outcome: Jesus boldly enters Galilee proclaiming, "This is the time . . . Repent, and believe." Temptations always force us to make a choice. Jesus' choice is to take up his saving mission. What is our temptation? What is our choice? These are *the* questions of Lent, questions we must constantly ask if we wish to participate in Jesus' saving mission, proclaiming by the choices we make that the Gospel determines who we are and how we act.

### Connecting the Responsorial Psalm to the Readings

Lent is a "time of fulfillment" (gospel) during which we are called to renew our covenant relationship (first reading) with God. In Psalm 25 we ask God to teach us the ways of the covenant and to guide us in truth. We beg God to remember us with compassion and kindness and to offer us gentle correction and steady guidance. By singing Psalm 25 we choose, as did Jesus in the desert (gospel), to make our covenant relationship with God the guiding force of our lives. May this Lent lead us to deeper understanding of God's covenant with us and deeper commitment to its ways of "love and truth."

### Psalmist Preparation

In this responsorial psalm you reflect on the meaning of the covenant and ask to be led toward more faithful observance of its ways. How is God calling you this Lent to deepen your living of the covenant? How will you, like Jesus in the desert, struggle with this call? Who or what will help you say yes?

### Prayer

Saving God, you offer us life and love. Lead us during this Lenten season to imitate your Son more fully that we may follow your will and walk in your ways. We ask this through him, our Brother and Savior. Amen.

### Gospel (Mark 9:2-10; L26B)

Jesus took Peter, James, and John and led them
up a high mountain apart by themselves.
And he was transfigured before them, and
his clothes became dazzling white, such as
no fuller on earth could bleach them.
Then Elijah appeared to them along
with Moses, and they were conversing
with Jesus. Then Peter said to Jesus in
reply, "Rabbi, it is good that we are here!
Let us make three tents: one for you, one
for Moses, and one for Elijah." He hardly
knew what to say, they were so terrified.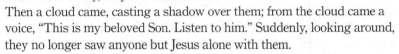
Then a cloud came, casting a shadow over them; from the cloud came a
voice, "This is my beloved Son. Listen to him." Suddenly, looking around,
they no longer saw anyone but Jesus alone with them.

As they were coming down from the mountain, he charged them not
to relate what they had seen to anyone, except when the Son of Man had
risen from the dead. So they kept the matter to themselves, questioning
what rising from the dead meant.

### First Reading (Gen 22:1-2, 9a, 10-13, 15-18)

God put Abraham to the test. He called to him, "Abraham!" "Here I am!"
he replied. Then God said: "Take your son Isaac, your only one, whom
you love, and go to the land of Moriah. There you shall offer him up as a
holocaust on a height that I will point out to you."

When they came to the place of which God had told him, Abraham
built an altar there and arranged the wood on it. Then he reached out and
took the knife to slaughter his son. But the LORD's messenger called to him
from heaven, "Abraham, Abraham!" "Here I am!" he answered. "Do not
lay your hand on the boy," said the messenger. "Do not do the least thing
to him. I know now how devoted you are to God, since you did not withhold from me your own beloved son." As Abraham looked about, he spied
a ram caught by its horns in the thicket. So he went and took the ram and
offered it up as a holocaust in place of his son.

Again the LORD's messenger called to Abraham from heaven and said:
"I swear by myself, declares the LORD, that because you acted as you did
in not withholding from me your beloved son, I will bless you abundantly
and make your descendants as countless as the stars of the sky and the

sands of the seashore; your descendants shall take possession of the gates of their enemies, and in your descendants all the nations of the earth shall find blessing—all this because you obeyed my command."

### Responsorial Psalm (Ps 116:10, 15, 16-17, 18-19)

℟. (116:9) I will walk before the Lord, in the land of the living.

I believed, even when I said,
   "I am greatly afflicted."
Precious in the eyes of the LORD
   is the death of his faithful ones.

℟. I will walk before the Lord, in the land of the living.

O LORD, I am your servant;
   I am your servant, the son of your handmaid;
   you have loosed my bonds.
To you will I offer sacrifice of thanksgiving,
   and I will call upon the name of the LORD.

℟. I will walk before the Lord, in the land of the living.

My vows to the LORD I will pay
   in the presence of all his people,
In the courts of the house of the LORD,
   in your midst, O Jerusalem.

℟. I will walk before the Lord, in the land of the living.

*See Appendix, p. 203, for Second Reading*

### Reflecting on Living the Gospel

On the mountain Peter, James, and John witness three theophanies (appearances of God): Jesus the transfigured One, Jesus the "beloved Son," Jesus the "Son of Man." Coming "down from the mountain," they would witness Jesus passing through death to the full revelation of what had been foreshadowed in his transfiguration: the theophany of his risen, glorified Body. Finally, when Peter, James, and John choose dying to self, they are transfigured by Jesus' risen Life. *They* too become theophanies. So can *we*.

### Connecting the Responsorial Psalm to the Readings

Psalm 116 was a psalm of thanksgiving sung to God after being delivered from death: "I will walk before the Lord, in the land of the living" (psalm refrain). We can easily place its words on Abraham's lips after the voice from heaven stayed the knife he held over Isaac (first reading). We can hear its words on the lips of Christ who, having died for our sakes, was raised to new life (second reading). What does it mean for us to place these words on our lips on the Second Sunday of Lent? We sing this psalm knowing that what God desires for us is life, not death. We sing this psalm also knowing that to receive the fuller life God wishes for us we must pass through whatever dying to self comes from listening to the call of God (first reading) and the voice of Jesus (gospel). Abraham listened and learned this. Peter, James, and John listened and learned this. Now is our time to listen and learn.

### Psalmist Preparation

To "walk before the Lord, in the land of the living" (psalm refrain) does not mean that you will never face death. On the contrary, the readings and gospel tell you just the opposite. Ask God this week for the grace you need to sing this psalm with the courage and the confidence it requires.

### Prayer

God of the living, you lead us through death to fuller life. During this Lenten season, grant us the courage we need to follow your Son to the cross that we might be transformed with him into glory. We ask this in his name. Amen.

**MARCH 8, 2015**

### Gospel (John 2:13-25; L29B)

Since the Passover of the Jews was near, Jesus went up to Jerusalem. He found in the temple area those who sold oxen, sheep, and doves, as well as the money changers seated there. He made a whip out of cords and drove them all out of the temple area, with the sheep and oxen, and spilled the coins of the money changers and overturned their tables, and to those who sold doves he said, "Take these out of here, and stop making my Father's house a marketplace." His disciples recalled the words of Scripture, *Zeal for your house will consume me.* At this the Jews answered and said to him, "What sign can you show us for doing this?" Jesus answered and said to them, "Destroy this temple and in three days I will raise it up." The Jews said, "This temple has been under construction for forty-six years, and you will raise it up in three days?" But he was speaking about the temple of his body. Therefore, when he was raised from the dead, his disciples remembered that he had said this, and they came to believe the Scripture and the word Jesus had spoken.

While he was in Jerusalem for the feast of Passover, many began to believe in his name when they saw the signs he was doing. But Jesus would not trust himself to them because he knew them all, and did not need anyone to testify about human nature. He himself understood it well.

### First Reading (Exod 20:1-17 [or Exod 20:1-3, 7-8, 12-17])

[In those days, God delivered all these commandments: "I, the LORD, am your God, who brought you out of the land of Egypt, that place of slavery. You shall not have other gods besides me.] You shall not carve idols for yourselves in the shape of anything in the sky above or on the earth below or in the waters beneath the earth; you shall not bow down before them or worship them. For I, the LORD, your God, am a jealous God, inflicting punishment for their fathers' wickedness on the children of those who hate me, down to the third and fourth generation; but bestowing mercy down to the thousandth generation on the children of those who love me and keep my commandments.

["You shall not take the name of the LORD, your God, in vain. For the LORD will not leave unpunished the one who takes his name in vain.

"Remember to keep holy the sabbath day.] Six days you may labor and do all your work, but the seventh day is the sabbath of the LORD, your God. No work may be done then either by you, or your son or daughter, or your male or female slave, or your beast, or by the alien who lives with you. In six days the LORD made the heavens and the earth, the sea and all that is in them; but on the seventh day he rested. That is why the LORD has blessed the sabbath day and made it holy.

["Honor your father and your mother, that you may have a long life in the land which the LORD, your God, is giving you.

You shall not kill.

You shall not commit adultery.

You shall not steal.

You shall not bear false witness against your neighbor.

You shall not covet your neighbor's house.

You shall not covet your neighbor's wife, nor his male or female slave, nor his ox or ass, nor anything else that belongs to him."]

### Responsorial Psalm (Ps 19:8, 9, 10, 11)

R̸. (John 6:68c) Lord, you have the words of everlasting life.

The law of the LORD is perfect,
    refreshing the soul;
The decree of the LORD is trustworthy,
    giving wisdom to the simple.

R̸. Lord, you have the words of everlasting life.

The precepts of the LORD are right,
    rejoicing the heart;
the command of the LORD is clear,
    enlightening the eye.

R̸. Lord, you have the words of everlasting life.

The fear of the LORD is pure,
    enduring forever;
the ordinances of the LORD are true,
    all of them just.

R̸. Lord, you have the words of everlasting life.

They are more precious than gold,
    than a heap of purest gold;
sweeter also than syrup
    or honey from the comb.

R̸. Lord, you have the words of everlasting life.

*See Appendix, p. 203, for Second Reading*

### Reflecting on Living the Gospel
The temple in Jerusalem was a sign to the Jews of God's Presence and saving works. This sign could be corrupted, however, by human beings who turn away from the temple's true purpose. Enraged, Jesus takes "a whip" and drives out of the temple area those who corrupt the sign. Then Jesus announces both a new temple (his own body) that could not be corrupted and a new sign ("raised from the dead"). Now *we* are the new temple: the living sign of the new things God is doing for us.

### Connecting the Responsorial Psalm to the Readings
Psalm 19, from which this responsorial psalm is taken, has three sections. The first (vv. 2-7) describes the sun joyfully running its course from one end of heaven to the other. Nothing escapes its heat. The second (vv. 8-11) sings the praise of God's Law from which all good comes. The third (vv. 12-15) is an acknowledgment of sin, both unconscious and willful, with a plea that God keep the psalmist faithful.

Just as the sun gives light to the earth, so does God's Law give light to humankind. Both leave no corners in shadow. Yet, how easily humans fail to live in this light. In the temple Jesus, who understands "human nature" well, confronts this love of darkness with directness and force (gospel). He is "the power . . . and the wisdom of God" (second reading) bringing the light of God's judgment to bear upon human behavior. He is God's Law personified. By singing these verses from Psalm 19, we tell him that we hear his "words of everlasting life" (psalm refrain) and will heed them.

### Psalmist Preparation
Read and reflect on the entirety of Psalm 19 as you prepare to sing the portion of it assigned for this Sunday's responsorial psalm. The comparison of God's Law to the light of the sun, and the honesty with which the psalmist prays to remain faithful to the Law reveal that the Law is

not a list of things to do or not do, but the roadmap to a loving relationship with God and neighbor. How was Jesus faithful to this Law? How is
he calling you to be faithful?

### Prayer

Saving God, you sent your Son to be our guide and wisdom on earth.
Lead us to walk always in the light of his judgment that we may gain
fullness of life. We ask this through him, our Brother and Savior. Amen.

### Gospel (John 3:14-21; L32B)

Jesus said to Nicodemus: "Just as Moses lifted up
the serpent in the desert, so must the Son of Man
be lifted up, so that everyone who believes in
him may have eternal life."

For God so loved the world that he gave
his only Son, so that everyone who believes
in him might not perish but might have eternal life. For
God did not send his Son into the world to condemn
the world, but that the world might be saved through
him. Whoever believes in him will not be condemned,
but whoever does not believe has already been condemned, because he has not believed in the name of
the only Son of God. And this is the verdict, that the
light came into the world, but people preferred darkness to light, because their works were evil. For everyone who does
wicked things hates the light and does not come toward the light, so that
his works might not be exposed. But whoever lives the truth comes to
the light, so that his works may be clearly seen as done in God.

### First Reading (2 Chr 36:14-16, 19-23)

In those days, all the princes of Judah, the priests, and the people added
infidelity to infidelity, practicing all the abominations of the nations and
polluting the LORD's temple which he had consecrated in Jerusalem.

Early and often did the LORD, the God of their fathers, send his messengers to them, for he had compassion on his people and his dwelling
place. But they mocked the messengers of God, despised his warnings,
and scoffed at his prophets, until the anger of the LORD against his
people was so inflamed that there was no remedy. Their enemies burnt
the house of God, tore down the walls of Jerusalem, set all its palaces
afire, and destroyed all its precious objects. Those who escaped the
sword were carried captive to Babylon, where they became servants of
the king of the Chaldeans and his sons until the kingdom of the Persians
came to power. All this was to fulfill the word of the LORD spoken by Jeremiah: "Until the land has retrieved its lost sabbaths, during all the time
it lies waste it shall have rest while seventy years are fulfilled."

In the first year of Cyrus, king of Persia, in order to fulfill the word
of the LORD spoken by Jeremiah, the LORD inspired King Cyrus of Persia
to issue this proclamation throughout his kingdom, both by word of

mouth and in writing: "Thus says Cyrus, king of Persia: All the kingdoms of the earth the LORD, the God of heaven, has given to me, and he has also charged me to build him a house in Jerusalem, which is in Judah. Whoever, therefore, among you belongs to any part of his people, let him go up, and may his God be with him!"

### Responsorial Psalm (Ps 137:1-2, 3, 4-5, 6)

R̸. (6ab) Let my tongue be silenced, if I ever forget you!

By the streams of Babylon
  we sat and wept
  when we remembered Zion.
On the aspens of that land
  we hung up our harps.

R̸. Let my tongue be silenced, if I ever forget you!

For there our captors asked of us
  the lyrics of our songs,
And our despoilers urged us to be joyous:
  "Sing for us the songs of Zion!"

R̸. Let my tongue be silenced, if I ever forget you!

How could we sing a song of the LORD
  in a foreign land?
If I forget you, Jerusalem,
  may my right hand be forgotten!

R̸. Let my tongue be silenced, if I ever forget you!

May my tongue cleave to my palate
  if I remember you not,
If I place not Jerusalem
  ahead of my joy.

R̸. Let my tongue be silenced, if I ever forget you!

*See Appendix, p. 203, for Second Reading*

### Reflecting on Living the Gospel

There are two parts to this gospel, separated by the line "And this is the verdict." The first part concerns the evidence: God "gave his only Son" in whom we choose to believe or not. The second part gives the judgment:

those are saved who believe in Jesus, live the truth, and come to the light. Those are condemned who do not believe in Jesus, prefer darkness, and do "wicked things." Our whole life is working out our own verdict. Thank God we are at the mercy of a gracious and forgiving God!

### Connecting the Responsorial Psalm to the Readings

This Sunday's responsorial psalm is difficult to understand unless we see it in the context of Israel's exile in Babylon. The exile was devastating and the Israelites had brought it upon themselves through their unfaithfulness to the covenant (first reading). Psalm 137 echoes the bitterness of the exile and is a reflection upon the utter barrenness of that experience. It is also a plea that the Israelites never again forget what it means to be God's chosen people.

The second reading tells us that we, too, have been restored to life "even when we were dead in our transgressions." The only Son of God came not to condemn but to save us (gospel). And, just as the Israelites, we must make a choice: to believe, to walk toward the light, to live the truth. The psalm challenges us to remember the price of forgetting what God has given us by sending the Son.

### Psalmist Preparation

When have you been in exile from God and the community? What led you there? What did this exile feel like? How did God mercifully bring you back home?

### Prayer

God, rich in mercy, you sent your Son to lead us from the exile of sin and death to renewed life. As he gave his life for our salvation so may we give our lives to you in love. We ask this through him, our Brother and Savior. Amen.

### Gospel (John 12:20-33; L35B)

Some Greeks who had come to worship at the Passover Feast came to Philip, who was from Bethsaida in Galilee, and asked him, "Sir, we would like to see Jesus." Philip went and told Andrew; then Andrew and Philip went and told Jesus. Jesus answered them, "The hour has come for the Son of Man to be glorified. Amen, amen, I say to you, unless a grain of wheat falls to the ground and dies, it remains just a grain of wheat; but if it dies, it produces much fruit. Whoever loves his life loses it, and whoever hates his life in this world will preserve it for eternal life. Whoever serves me must follow me, and where I am, there also will my servant be. The Father will honor whoever serves me.

"I am troubled now. Yet what should I say? 'Father, save me from this hour'? But it was for this purpose that I came to this hour. Father, glorify your name." Then a voice came from heaven, "I have glorified it and will glorify it again." The crowd there heard it and said it was thunder; but others said, "An angel has spoken to him." Jesus answered and said, "This voice did not come for my sake but for yours. Now is the time of judgment on this world; now the ruler of this world will be driven out. And when I am lifted up from the earth, I will draw everyone to myself." He said this indicating the kind of death he would die.

### First Reading (Jer 31:31-34)

The days are coming, says the LORD, when I will make a new covenant with the house of Israel and the house of Judah. It will not be like the covenant I made with their fathers the day I took them by the hand to lead them forth from the land of Egypt; for they broke my covenant, and I had to show myself their master, says the LORD. But this is the covenant that I will make with the house of Israel after those days, says the LORD. I will place my law within them and write it upon their hearts; I will be their God, and they shall be my people. No longer will they have need to teach their friends and relatives how to know the LORD. All, from least to greatest, shall know me, says the LORD, for I will forgive their evildoing and remember their sin no more.

**Responsorial Psalm (Ps 51:3-4, 12-13, 14-15)**

R℣. (12a) Create a clean heart in me, O God.

Have mercy on me, O God, in your goodness;
in the greatness of your compassion wipe out my offense.
Thoroughly wash me from my guilt
and of my sin cleanse me.

R℣. Create a clean heart in me, O God.

A clean heart create for me, O God,
and a steadfast spirit renew within me.
Cast me not out from your presence,
and your Holy Spirit take not from me.

R℣. Create a clean heart in me, O God.

Give me back the joy of your salvation,
and a willing spirit sustain in me.
I will teach transgressors your ways,
and sinners shall return to you.

R℣. Create a clean heart in me, O God.

*See Appendix, p. 203, for Second Reading*

### Reflecting on Living the Gospel

Jesus reveals his "hour . . . to be glorified" in surprisingly inglorious ways: dying grain, losing life, serving others. Jesus himself struggled with this: "I am troubled now." When we focus only on the giving up and the giving over of our lives, we fail to take into account the glorification. The Father is glorified in the very giving over of the Son. The Son is glorified in giving himself over to the cross. We are glorified in giving ourselves over to following Jesus to the cross. And this glorification is fullness of Life.

### Connecting the Responsorial Psalm to the Readings

Often in the psalms, a person confronted with suffering claims innocence of any evildoing which could have caused the suffering (see Psalm 26, for example). In Psalm 51, however, the person praying readily acknowledges guilt. Moreover, the person begs not just to be forgiven but to be completely transformed. The very praying of Psalm 51, then, brings about a dying to self and a rising to new life.

In the first reading God offers us a new covenant, a new life, a new heart. In Psalm 51 we acknowledge our need for this transformation and ask God to do it. The good news is that our transformation has already been accomplished through Christ who freely chose death that he might bear the fruit of new life for us (first reading, gospel). When we sing Psalm 51 this Sunday, we open our hearts to receive what he has done for us. We acknowledge who we are—sinners in need of redemption—and receive who we have become because of him, a community filled with the joy of salvation (psalm).

### Psalmist Preparation

Singing these verses from Psalm 51 requires honesty about your own sinfulness and need for forgiveness. Arriving at such honesty is painful, but it is also a moment of resurrection, for it opens your heart to receive God's merciful forgiveness. Psalm 51 sings about the "ways" of God; singing Psalm 51 *is* the way to God.

### Prayer

Saving God, you embrace the sinner who turns to you for mercy. Lead us back to you that we may be given clean hearts ready to do your will. We ask this through Christ our Lord. Amen.

*Gospel at the procession with palms*
**(Mark 11:1-10 or John 12:12-16; L37B)**

*Gospel at Mass*
**(Mark 14:1–15:47; L38B)**

### *First Reading* (Isa 50:4-7)

The Lord GOD has given me
a well-trained tongue,
that I might know how to
speak to the weary
a word that will rouse them.
Morning after morning
he opens my ear that I may hear;
and I have not rebelled,
have not turned back.
I gave my back to those who beat me,
my cheeks to those who plucked my beard;
my face I did not shield
from buffets and spitting.

The Lord GOD is my help,
therefore I am not disgraced;
I have set my face like flint,
knowing that I shall not be put to shame.

### *Responsorial Psalm* (Ps 22:8-9, 17-18, 19-20, 23-24)

℟. (2a) My God, my God, why have you abandoned me?
All who see me scoff at me;
they mock me with parted lips, they wag their heads:
"He relied on the LORD; let him deliver him,
let him rescue him, if he loves him."

℟. My God, my God, why have you abandoned me?
Indeed, many dogs surround me,
a pack of evildoers closes in upon me;
they have pierced my hands and my feet;
I can count all my bones.

℟. My God, my God, why have you abandoned me?

They divide my garments among them,
    and for my vesture they cast lots.
But you, O LORD, be not far from me;
    O my help, hasten to aid me.

R̸. My God, my God, why have you abandoned me?

I will proclaim your name to my brethren;
    in the midst of the assembly I will praise you:
"You who fear the LORD, praise him;
    all you descendants of Jacob, give glory to him;
    revere him, all you descendants of Israel!"

R̸. My God, my God, why have you abandoned me?

*See Appendix, p. 203, for Second Reading*

### Reflecting on Living the Gospel
In Mark's account of Jesus' passion, many persons respond to Jesus in
many different ways. At the Last Supper, Peter and the rest of the
Twelve swear they will never deny him. Judas betrays Jesus with a kiss.
Peter denies Jesus three times. Soldiers mock him. Soldiers crucify him.
The centurion proclaims Jesus to be the "Son of God." During Jesus' last
hours, only a few faithful people stand by Jesus. Most do not. As we hear
this passion proclaimed, where do we stand?

### Connecting the Responsorial Psalm to the Readings
The Lectionary uses only a few verses of Psalm 22, and reading the
whole psalm gives us a fuller understanding of why the church has traditionally used this psalm on Palm Sunday of the Lord's Passion. The
psalm contains three thematic progressions. The first progression (vv.
12-17) is that of abandonment, first by God, then by fellow human beings, until finally the psalmist is surrounded by ravening animals. The
second progression emerges simultaneously, but in the opposite direction. The distant God who has abandoned the psalmist (vv. 2-3) becomes
an intimate God who has known us from birth (v. 11). The third progression (vv. 23-32) is a prayer of praise and thanksgiving into which an
ever-widening circle is invited to participate: immediate family, the offspring of Jacob, all nations, generations yet unborn, all the ends of the
earth, the afflicted, the poor, and even the dead. The praise is eschatological and cosmic. These thematic progressions transform our response

to the proclamation of the passion. We are doing more than telling a story about abandonment and death, more than remembering the pain of Christ on the cross. We are joining Christ in his song of praise and thanksgiving. We are entering into the mystery of our salvation.

### Psalmist Preparation

The few verses of Psalm 22 used this Sunday offer only a glimpse of the psalm's depth and of its connection with the meaning of what the church celebrates during Holy Week. Spend some time this week praying the entirety of Psalm 22, and ask for the grace to enter fully with Jesus into the paschal mystery of death and resurrection, of God's absence and God's nearness, of suffering and praise.

### Prayer

Redeeming God, you sent your Son to teach us that we overcome death by willingly accepting it for the sake of others. Be with us as we enter this holiest week of the year. Give us the courage we need to walk with Jesus to the cross and to the glory beyond. We ask this through him, our Brother and Savior. Amen.

### *Gospel* (John 13:1-15; L39ABC)

Before the feast of Passover, Jesus knew that his hour had come to pass from this world to the Father. He loved his own in the world and he loved them to the end. The devil had already induced Judas, son of Simon the Iscariot, to hand him over. So, during supper, fully aware that the Father had put everything into his power and that he had come from God and was returning to God, he rose from supper and took off his outer garments. He took a towel and tied it around his waist. Then he poured water into a basin and began to wash the disciples' feet and dry them with the towel around his waist. He came to Simon Peter, who said to him, "Master, are you going to wash my feet?" Jesus answered and said to him, "What I am doing, you do not understand now, but you will understand later." Peter said to him, "You will never wash my feet." Jesus answered him, "Unless I wash you, you will have no inheritance with me." Simon Peter said to him, "Master, then not only my feet, but my hands and head as well." Jesus said to him, "Whoever has bathed has no need except to have his feet washed, for he is clean all over; so you are clean, but not all." For he knew who would betray him; for this reason, he said, "Not all of you are clean."

So when he had washed their feet and put his garments back on and reclined at table again, he said to them, "Do you realize what I have done for you? You call me 'teacher' and 'master,' and rightly so, for indeed I am. If I, therefore, the master and teacher, have washed your feet, you ought to wash one another's feet. I have given you a model to follow, so that as I have done for you, you should also do."

### *First Reading* (Exod 12:1-8, 11-14)

The LORD said to Moses and Aaron in the land of Egypt, "This month shall stand at the head of your calendar; you shall reckon it the first month of the year. Tell the whole community of Israel: On the tenth of this month every one of your families must procure for itself a lamb, one apiece for each household. If a family is too small for a whole lamb, it shall join the nearest household in procuring one and shall share in the lamb in proportion to the number of persons who partake of it. The lamb must be a year-old male and without blemish. You may take it from either the sheep or the goats. You shall keep it until the fourteenth day of this month, and then, with the whole assembly of Israel present, it shall be slaughtered during the evening twilight. They shall take some of its blood and apply it to the two doorposts and the lintel of every house in which they partake of the lamb. That same night they shall eat its roasted flesh with unleavened bread and bitter herbs.

"This is how you are to eat it: with your loins girt, sandals on your feet and your staff in hand, you shall eat like those who are in flight. It is the Passover of the LORD. For on this same night I will go through Egypt, striking down every firstborn of the land, both man and beast, and executing judgment on all the gods of Egypt—I, the LORD! But the blood will mark the houses where you are. Seeing the blood, I will pass over you; thus, when I strike the land of Egypt, no destructive blow will come upon you.

"This day shall be a memorial feast for you, which all your generations shall celebrate with pilgrimage to the LORD, as a perpetual institution."

### Responsorial Psalm (Ps 116:12-13, 15-16bc, 17-18)

R︎. (cf. 1 Cor 10:16) Our blessing-cup is a communion with the Blood of Christ.

How shall I make a return to the LORD
   for all the good he has done for me?
The cup of salvation I will take up,
   and I will call upon the name of the LORD.

R︎. Our blessing-cup is a communion with the Blood of Christ.

Precious in the eyes of the LORD
   is the death of his faithful ones.
I am your servant, the son of your handmaid;
   you have loosed my bonds.

R︎. Our blessing-cup is a communion with the Blood of Christ.

To you will I offer sacrifice of thanksgiving,
   and I will call upon the name of the LORD.
My vows to the LORD I will pay
   in the presence of all his people.

R︎. Our blessing-cup is a communion with the Blood of Christ.

# HOLY THURSDAY EVENING MASS OF THE LORD'S SUPPER

*See Appendix, p. 204, for Second Reading*

### Reflecting on Living the Gospel

Jesus gave us a profound witness to what self-giving love looks like: he washed his disciples' feet. This act of humble service is our "model to follow." We wash the feet of others when we love with the same kind of unreserved love as Jesus showed us. This footwashing is more than a ritual act. It is a way of living and loving. This sums up all Jesus taught. This sums up the meaning of the Supper. This sums up this night. This sums up Jesus' whole life. So must it sum up ours.

### Connecting the Responsorial Psalm to the Readings

The "blessing-cup" about which we sing in the psalm refrain was the third cup drunk as part of the Jewish Passover meal. Those who shared this cup were united with each other and God. On Holy Thursday—and at every celebration of the Eucharist—the "blessing-cup" we drink is the Blood of Christ, source of our salvation. By drinking this cup we take the Blood of Christ into ourselves and become one with him in his death and resurrection. Drinking this cup does not save us *from* death but *through* death, a death freely chosen in self-giving service to one another (gospel). By drinking it we not only "proclaim the death of the Lord" (second reading), we unite ourselves with him and with one another in his death, and find salvation.

### Psalmist Preparation

What are the "vows to the LORD" you pay in drinking the blessing-cup of Christ's Blood? Certainly, you thank God for saving your life through Christ. But you also promise to become one with Christ in losing your life for the sake of others. You promise to become the servant who washes feet. Are you willing to do this? Whose feet need washing?

### Prayer

Redeeming God, you call us to communion in the Blood of Christ. May our drinking of his cup lead us always to serve one another in generous and joyful love. We ask this in his name. Amen.

*Gospel* (John 18:1–19:42; L40ABC)

*First Reading* (Isa 52:13–53:12)

See, my servant shall prosper,
   he shall be raised high and greatly exalted.
Even as many were amazed
      at him—
   so marred was his look beyond human
         semblance
   and his appearance beyond that of the sons
         of man—
so shall he startle many nations,
   because of him kings shall stand speechless;
for those who have not been told shall see,
   those who have not heard shall ponder it.

Who would believe what we have heard?
   To whom has the arm of the LORD been revealed?
He grew up like a sapling before him,
   like a shoot from the parched earth;
there was in him no stately bearing to make us look at him,
   nor appearance that would attract us to him.
He was spurned and avoided by people,
   a man of suffering, accustomed to infirmity,
one of those from whom people hide their faces,
   spurned, and we held him in no esteem.

Yet it was our infirmities that he bore,
   our sufferings that he endured,
while we thought of him as stricken,
   as one smitten by God and afflicted.
But he was pierced for our offenses,
   crushed for our sins;
upon him was the chastisement that makes us whole,
   by his stripes we were healed.
We had all gone astray like sheep,
   each following his own way;
but the LORD laid upon him
   the guilt of us all.

Though he was harshly treated, he submitted
    and opened not his mouth;
like a lamb led to the slaughter
    or a sheep before the shearers,
    he was silent and opened not his mouth.
Oppressed and condemned, he was taken away,
    and who would have thought any more of his destiny?
When he was cut off from the land of the living,
    and smitten for the sin of his people,
a grave was assigned him among the wicked
    and a burial place with evildoers,
though he had done no wrong
    nor spoken any falsehood.
But the LORD was pleased
    to crush him in infirmity.

If he gives his life as an offering for sin,
    he shall see his descendants in a long life,
    and the will of the LORD shall be accomplished through him.

Because of his affliction
    he shall see the light
        in fullness of days;
through his suffering, my servant shall justify many,
    and their guilt he shall bear.
Therefore I will give him his portion among the great,
    and he shall divide the spoils with the mighty,
because he surrendered himself to death
    and was counted among the wicked;
and he shall take away the sins of many,
    and win pardon for their offenses.

### Responsorial Psalm (Ps 31:2, 6, 12-13, 15-16, 17, 25)

R. (Luke 23:46) Father, into your hands I commend my spirit.

In you, O LORD, I take refuge;
    let me never be put to shame.
In your justice rescue me.
Into your hands I commend my spirit;
    you will redeem me, O LORD, O faithful God.

R. Father, into your hands I commend my spirit.

For all my foes I am an object of reproach,
    a laughingstock to my neighbors, and a dread to my friends;
    they who see me abroad flee from me.
I am forgotten like the unremembered dead;
    I am like a dish that is broken.

R℣. Father, into your hands I commend my spirit.

But my trust is in you, O Lᴏʀᴅ;
    I say, "You are my God.
In your hands is my destiny; rescue me
    from the clutches of my enemies and my persecutors."

R℣. Father, into your hands I commend my spirit.

Let your face shine upon your servant;
    save me in your kindness.
Take courage and be stouthearted,
    all you who hope in the Lᴏʀᴅ.

R℣. Father, into your hands I commend my spirit.

*See Appendix, p. 204, for Second Reading*

### Reflecting on Living the Gospel

Jesus accepted mockery and rejection rather than compromise the goodness he was. He accepted suffering and death as a climactic act of fidelity and love. He "handed over the spirit" in an awe-inspiring act of self-giving. Even after death, he poured forth "blood and water" from his side, foreshadowing our own baptismal entry into his mystery and our participation in his perpetual self-giving in the eucharistic sacrifice. On this "Good" Friday we are invited to choose good. We are invited to embrace Jesus' self-giving love.

### Connecting the Responsorial Psalm to the Readings

Psalm 31 is a poignant lament in which someone persecuted by enemies calls trustfully to God for help, then sings thanksgiving to God for salvation. Onlookers consider this person a fool ("laughingstock"), fearful to look at ("a dread"), someone best "forgotten." But to God this person is a faithful servant for whom God will always be faithful Redeemer. The Lectionary places words from Psalm 31 on the lips of Jesus, and frames his prayer with the refrain, "Father, into your hands I commend my spirit." Jesus' "spirit" is both his life-breath and the orientation of his heart. Amidst the unspeakable sufferings of his passion and death he continues to surrender himself, as he did all his life, to the Father in whose presence and care he trusts. The final verse stands as Jesus' words to us, and our words to all who remain faithful to God no matter what the personal cost: "Take courage . . . hope in the LORD."

### Psalmist Preparation

You sing these words from Psalm 31 as one united with Jesus in his gift of self to the Father. In your singing you invite assembly members also to join themselves with Jesus. You encourage them in the final verse to remain "stouthearted" in their hope in the God of life and salvation. What keeps you stouthearted? How at this moment in your life do you need to give yourself over in obedience and trust to God? What gives you the courage to do so?

### Prayer

God of salvation, in the life, death, and resurrection of your Son Jesus, you give over your Spirit to us. Open our hearts that, united with Jesus, we may return your gift by offering our spirit to you in obedience, trust, and love. We ask this through him, our Brother and Savior. Amen.

**APRIL 4, 2015**

*Additional readings can be found in the Lectionary for Mass.*

### Gospel (Mark 16:1-7; L41B)

When the sabbath was over, Mary Magdalene, Mary, the mother of James, and Salome bought spices so that they might go and anoint him. Very early when the sun had risen, on the first day of the week, they came to the tomb. They were saying to one another, "Who will roll back the stone for us from the entrance to the tomb?" When they looked up, they saw that the stone had been rolled back; it was very large. On entering the tomb they saw a young man sitting on the right side, clothed in a white robe, and they were utterly amazed. He said to them, "Do not be amazed! You seek Jesus of Nazareth, the crucified. He has been raised; he is not here. Behold the place where they laid him. But go and tell his disciples and Peter, 'He is going before you to Galilee; there you will see him, as he told you.'"

### *Epistle (Rom 6:3-11)*

Brothers and sisters: Are you unaware that we who were baptized into Christ Jesus were baptized into his death? We were indeed buried with him through baptism into death, so that, just as Christ was raised from the dead by the glory of the Father, we too might live in newness of life.

For if we have grown into union with him through a death like his, we shall also be united with him in the resurrection. We know that our old self was crucified with him, so that our sinful body might be done away with, that we might no longer be in slavery to sin. For a dead person has been absolved from sin. If, then, we have died with Christ, we believe that we shall also live with him. We know that Christ, raised from the dead, dies no more; death no longer has power over him. As to his death, he died to sin once and for all; as to his life, he lives for God. Consequently, you too must think of yourselves as being dead to sin and living for God in Christ Jesus.

### Responsorial Psalm (Ps 118:1-2, 16-17, 22-23)

R̸. Alleluia, alleluia, alleluia.

Give thanks to the LORD, for he is good,
    for his mercy endures forever.
Let the house of Israel say,
    "His mercy endures forever."

R̸. Alleluia, alleluia, alleluia.

"The right hand of the LORD has struck with power;
    the right hand of the LORD is exalted.
I shall not die, but live,
    and declare the works of the LORD."

R̸. Alleluia, alleluia, alleluia.

The stone which the builders rejected
    has become the cornerstone.
By the LORD has this been done;
    it is wonderful in our eyes.

R̸. Alleluia, alleluia, alleluia.

### Reflecting on Living the Gospel

This night invites us to be at home. Be comfortable. Open ourselves to an encounter like no other we have ever had. We know what we also find in our midst: Jesus the risen One. Not in Galilee, but right here among us. This Jesus cannot be contained in a tomb. We do not visit a cemetery to encounter him. This Jesus has been raised from the dead and seeks us out, offers us new Life, prepares us to open ourselves to beauty, peace, and quiet like we have never before experienced.

### Connecting the Responsorial Psalm to the Readings

Psalm 118 was a hymn sung as the Israelites processed into the temple to give thanks to God for saving them from destruction by an enemy. The procession entailed a march through the streets during which a soloist sang verses about facing death and a choir responded with verses about God's intervention to save. Verses 14, 15-16 are drawn from Exodus 15, indicating the Israelites saw every victory over an enemy as an extension of the exodus event when God led them from slavery to freedom.

Psalm 118 is also our song of deliverance. Our saving event comes in Christ with whom we have died and risen, and with whom we share glory (epistle). Our call is to believe what has happened to Christ (gospel) and become aware of what has happened to us (epistle). As we sing Psalm 118, Christ is the soloist leading the song and we are the ones answering "Alleluia!"

### Psalmist Preparation

Are you unaware that you have died and risen with Christ (see epistle)? You proclaim to the assembly the wonderful work done by God in Christ and also done in them. How might you communicate the joy you feel this day both for yourself and for them?

### Prayer

Saving God, you raise us out of the darkness of sin and death to new life in your Son. May we always declare your saving works and live fully aware of what you have achieved in us. We ask this in his name. Amen.

# EASTER SUNDAY OF THE RESURRECTION

### Gospel (John 20:1-9; L42ABC)

On the first day of the week, Mary of Magdala came to the tomb early in the morning, while it was still dark, and saw the stone removed from the tomb. So she ran and went to Simon Peter and to the other disciple whom Jesus loved, and told them, "They have taken the Lord from the tomb, and we don't know where they put him." So Peter and the other disciple went out and came to the tomb. They both ran, but the other disciple ran faster than Peter and arrived at the tomb first; he bent down and saw the burial cloths there, but did not go in. When Simon Peter arrived after him, he went into the tomb and saw the burial cloths there, and the cloth that had covered his head, not with the burial cloths but rolled up in a separate place. Then the other disciple also went in, the one who had arrived at the tomb first, and he saw and believed. For they did not yet understand the Scripture that he had to rise from the dead.

### or Gospel (Mark 16:1-7; L41B)

### or at an afternoon or evening Mass
### Gospel (Luke 24:13-35; L46)

### First Reading (Acts 10:34a, 37-43)

Peter proceeded to speak and said: "You know what has happened all over Judea, beginning in Galilee after the baptism that John preached, how God anointed Jesus of Nazareth with the Holy Spirit and power. He went about doing good and healing all those oppressed by the devil, for God was with him. We are witnesses of all that he did both in the country of the Jews and in Jerusalem. They put him to death by hanging him on a tree. This man God raised on the third day and granted that he be visible, not to all the people, but to us, the witnesses chosen by God in advance, who ate and drank with him after he rose from the dead. He commissioned us to preach to the people and testify that he is the one appointed by God as judge of the living and the dead. To him all the prophets bear witness, that everyone who believes in him will receive forgiveness of sins through his name."

### Responsorial Psalm (Ps 118:1-2, 16-17, 22-23)

R̥. (24) This is the day the Lord has made; let us rejoice and be glad.
*or:* R̥. Alleluia.

Give thanks to the LORD, for he is good,
    for his mercy endures forever.
Let the house of Israel say,
    "His mercy endures forever."

R̥. This is the day the Lord has made; let us rejoice and be glad.
*or:* R̥. Alleluia.

"The right hand of the LORD has struck with power;
    the right hand of the LORD is exalted.
I shall not die, but live,
    and declare the works of the LORD."

R̥. This is the day the Lord has made; let us rejoice and be glad.
*or:* R̥. Alleluia.

The stone which the builders rejected
    has become the cornerstone.
By the LORD has this been done;
    it is wonderful in our eyes.

R̥. This is the day the Lord has made; let us rejoice and be glad.
*or:* R̥. Alleluia.

*See Appendix, p. 204, for Second Reading*

### Reflecting on Living the Gospel

The news of an empty tomb spread from Mary to Peter and the disciple.
They ran—hope quickens us. They believed—faith urges us. They witnessed to the good news—good news cannot be contained. Good news is infectious. Good news brings radiance to tired, suffering, worn faces. Good news such as an empty tomb and soon an encounter with the risen One not only cannot be contained, it changes us. Our own encounters with the risen One compel us to be witnesses, to spread Easter joy.

### Connecting the Responsorial Psalm to the Readings

Psalm 118 was a hymn sung as the Israelites processed into the temple to give thanks to God for saving them from destruction by an enemy. The procession entailed a march through the streets during which a soloist sang verses about facing death and a choir responded with verses about God's intervention to save. Verses 14, 15-16 are drawn from Exodus 15, indicating the Israelites saw every victory over an enemy as an extension of the exodus event when God led them from slavery to freedom.

Psalm 118 is also our song of deliverance. In the risen Christ, we have become a fresh batch of dough; old ways of malice have been replaced by a new life of sincerity and truth (second reading from 1 Corinthians). Our mission is to proclaim this work of God to all peoples (first reading). In singing Psalm 118 we do just that, calling all to rejoice in God's wonderful deeds.

### Psalmist Preparation

In Psalm 118, the source of the responsorial psalm for Easter Sunday, a choir led the Israelites processing into the temple in their praise for God's mighty acts of salvation. This is your role, not only on Easter but every Sunday. In order to sing of God's saving deeds, however, you must know what they are. How have you experienced death and resurrection this Lent? How has your family experienced it? your parish? the world?

### Prayer

All-powerful God, you raised your Son Jesus from the darkness of the tomb to the brightness of new life. Keep us united with him so that we, too, may be raised from death to new life. We ask this through him, our Brother and Savior. Amen.

### Gospel (John 20:19-31; L44B)

On the evening of that first day of the week, when the doors were locked, where the disciples were, for fear of the Jews, Jesus came and stood in their midst and said to them, "Peace be with you." When he had said this, he showed them his hands and his side. The disciples rejoiced when they saw the Lord. Jesus said to them again, "Peace be with you. As the Father has sent me, so I send you." And when he had said this, he breathed on them and said to them, "Receive the Holy Spirit. Whose sins you forgive are forgiven them, and whose sins you retain are retained."

Thomas, called Didymus, one of the Twelve, was not with them when Jesus came. So the other disciples said to him, "We have seen the Lord." But he said to them, "Unless I see the mark of the nails in his hands and put my finger into the nailmarks and put my hand into his side, I will not believe."

Now a week later his disciples were again inside and Thomas was with them. Jesus came, although the doors were locked, and stood in their midst and said, "Peace be with you." Then he said to Thomas, "Put your finger here and see my hands, and bring your hand and put it into my side, and do not be unbelieving, but believe." Thomas answered and said to him, "My Lord and my God!" Jesus said to him, "Have you come to believe because you have seen me? Blessed are those who have not seen and have believed."

Now Jesus did many other signs in the presence of his disciples that are not written in this book. But these are written that you may come to believe that Jesus is the Christ, the Son of God, and that through this belief you may have life in his name.

### First Reading (Acts 4:32-35)

The community of believers was of one heart and mind, and no one claimed that any of his possessions was his own, but they had everything in common. With great power the apostles bore witness to the resurrection of the Lord Jesus, and great favor was accorded them all. There was no needy person among them, for those who owned property or houses would sell them, bring the proceeds of the sale, and put them at the feet of the apostles, and they were distributed to each according to need.

**Responsorial Psalm (Ps 118:2-4, 13-15, 22-24)**

R⁊. (1) Give thanks to the Lord for he is good, his love is everlasting.
*or:* R⁊. Alleluia.

Let the house of Israel say,
 "His mercy endures forever."
Let the house of Aaron say,
 "His mercy endures forever."
Let those who fear the LORD say,
 "His mercy endures forever."

R⁊. Give thanks to the Lord for he is good, his love is everlasting.
*or:* R⁊. Alleluia.

I was hard pressed and was falling,
 but the LORD helped me.
My strength and my courage is the LORD,
 and he has been my savior.
The joyful shout of victory
 in the tents of the just.

R⁊. Give thanks to the Lord for he is good, his love is everlasting.
*or:* R⁊. Alleluia.

The stone which the builders rejected
 has become the cornerstone.
By the LORD has this been done;
 it is wonderful in our eyes.
This is the day the LORD has made;
 let us be glad and rejoice in it.

R⁊. Give thanks to the Lord for he is good, his love is everlasting.
*or:* R⁊. Alleluia.

*See Appendix, p. 204, for Second Reading*

### Reflecting on Living the Gospel

On Easter evening, the risen Jesus appears and shows the disciples "his hands and his side." It is Jesus who makes the first, convincing move to enable the disciples to believe that he has truly risen from the dead. It is he who wants the disciples to see him, to regain their confidence and peace. He bears the marks of suffering and death. Yet he is risen; he has conquered death. For himself and for all of us.

### Connecting the Responsorial Psalm to the Readings

Psalm 118 was a processional song in which the Israelites praised God for having saved them from destruction by an enemy. The psalm began with a call to worship and then continued as the people marched through Jerusalem to the temple. A soloist sang about facing death with confidence in God and a choir responded by singing about God's saving intervention. The rejected stone become the cornerstone may have referred to Israel itself, a puny nation considered easy to conquer by more powerful enemies. Or it may have referred to the stone of the temple, symbol of God, the rock of salvation.

Christian tradition applies the image to the risen Christ (Matt 21:42; Acts 4:11; 1 Pet 2:7). He is the foundation of our faith, the bedrock of our discipleship, the basis of our love for one another (second reading) and our care for the needy (first reading). He is the source of our victory over sin and death. In Psalm 118, we sing our joy and thanksgiving to the God who has made this happen.

### Psalmist Preparation

In this responsorial psalm you lead the assembly in praising God for the victory granted us in the risen Christ. Spend time this week giving God thanks. One way of doing this is to sing the psalm refrain as part of your personal prayer every day.

### Prayer

Redeeming God, make us signs of your saving love to all whom we meet, that we may lead them by our very manner of living to belief in your risen Son. We ask this in his name. Amen.

### *Gospel* (Luke 24:35-48; L47B)

The two disciples recounted what had taken place on the way, and how Jesus was made known to them in the breaking of bread.

While they were still speaking about this, he stood in their midst and said to them, "Peace be with you." But they were startled and terrified and thought that they were seeing a ghost. Then he said to them, "Why are you troubled? And why do questions arise in your hearts? Look at my hands and my feet, that it is I myself. Touch me and see, because a ghost does not have flesh and bones as you can see I have." And as he said this, he showed them his hands and his feet. While they were still incredulous for joy and were amazed, he asked them, "Have you anything here to eat?" They gave him a piece of baked fish; he took it and ate it in front of them.

He said to them, "These are my words that I spoke to you while I was still with you, that everything written about me in the law of Moses and in the prophets and psalms must be fulfilled." Then he opened their minds to understand the Scriptures. And he said to them, "Thus it is written that the Christ would suffer and rise from the dead on the third day and that repentance, for the forgiveness of sins, would be preached in his name to all the nations, beginning from Jerusalem. You are witnesses of these things."

### *First Reading* (Acts 3:13-15, 17-19)

Peter said to the people: "The God of Abraham, the God of Isaac, and the God of Jacob, the God of our fathers, has glorified his servant Jesus, whom you handed over and denied in Pilate's presence when he had decided to release him. You denied the Holy and Righteous One and asked that a murderer be released to you. The author of life you put to death, but God raised him from the dead; of this we are witnesses. Now I know, brothers, that you acted out of ignorance, just as your leaders did; but God has thus brought to fulfillment what he had announced beforehand through the mouth of all the prophets, that his Christ would suffer. Repent, therefore, and be converted, that your sins may be wiped away."

### Responsorial Psalm (Ps 4:2, 4, 7-8, 9)

℟. (7a) Lord, let your face shine on us. *or:* ℟. Alleluia.

When I call, answer me, O my just God,
  you who relieve me when I am in distress;
  have pity on me, and hear my prayer!

℟. Lord, let your face shine on us. *or:* ℟. Alleluia.

Know that the LORD does wonders for his faithful one;
  the LORD will hear me when I call upon him.

℟. Lord, let your face shine on us. *or:* ℟. Alleluia.

O LORD, let the light of your countenance shine upon us!
  You put gladness into my heart.

℟. Lord, let your face shine on us. *or:* ℟. Alleluia.

As soon as I lie down, I fall peacefully asleep,
  for you alone, O LORD,
  bring security to my dwelling.

℟. Lord, let your face shine on us. *or:* ℟. Alleluia.

*See Appendix, p. 205, for Second Reading*

### Reflecting on Living the Gospel

Jesus opened the minds of the disciples to grasp two things written in
the Scriptures: that he "would suffer and rise from the dead," and that
"repentance, for the forgiveness of sins, would be preached in his name
to all the nations." Our repentance—conversion of life—turns us to the
God who forgives and who fills us with the new Life of the resurrection.
Ultimately, this risen Life within us empowers a way of living that witnesses to God's forgiveness of our sinfulness.

### Connecting the Responsorial Psalm to the Readings

Psalm 4 is a lament begging God for mercy in a time of distress. The
psalm promises God will hear this cry for help and transform distress
into gladness, disturbance into peaceful sleep. Such a lament seems mis-
placed on the Third Sunday of Easter when we are well into our celebration of the mystery of the resurrection. But the readings and gospel
place this psalm in an Easter context. The situation of distress in Psalm 4

is our sinfulness; what transforms our situation is God's saving forgiveness; what reveals both human sinfulness and divine forgiveness is the death and resurrection of Jesus. Most importantly, it is God's forgiveness that pervades and prevails. This, the risen Jesus commands us, is what we are to preach to every corner of the world.

### Psalmist Preparation

In the context of this Sunday's readings and gospel, you pray in this psalm for the transformation that comes through the forgiveness of sins. You pray knowing that God shines the divine face of forgiveness upon us in the body of the risen Jesus. How might you turn to that Face? How might your face shine in response?

### Prayer

Glorious God, you shine your face upon us in the face of your risen Son. May our faces reflect his glory, and your love, so that all whom we meet may see your forgiveness and receive the peace you offer. We ask this through him, our Brother and Savior. Amen.

### *Gospel* (John 10:11-18; L50B)

Jesus said: "I am the good shepherd. A good shepherd lays down his life for the sheep. A hired man, who is not a shepherd and whose sheep are not his own, sees a wolf coming and leaves the sheep and runs away, and the wolf catches and scatters them. This is because he works for pay and has no concern for the sheep. I am the good shepherd, and I know mine and mine know me, just as the Father knows me and I know the Father; and I will lay down my life for the sheep. I have other sheep that do not belong to this fold. These also I must lead, and they will hear my voice, and there will be one flock, one shepherd. This is why the Father loves me, because I lay down my life in order to take it up again. No one takes it from me, but I lay it down on my own. I have power to lay it down, and power to take it up again. This command I have received from my Father."

### *First Reading* (Acts 4:8-12)

Peter, filled with the Holy Spirit, said: "Leaders of the people and elders: If we are being examined today about a good deed done to a cripple, namely, by what means he was saved, then all of you and all the people of Israel should know that it was in the name of Jesus Christ the Nazorean whom you crucified, whom God raised from the dead; in his name this man stands before you healed. He is *the stone rejected by you, the builders, which has become the cornerstone.* There is no salvation through anyone else, nor is there any other name under heaven given to the human race by which we are to be saved."

**Responsorial Psalm (Ps 118:1, 8-9, 21-23, 26, 28, 29)**

℟. (22) The stone rejected by the builders has become the cornerstone.
*or:* ℟. Alleluia.

Give thanks to the LORD, for he is good,
    for his mercy endures forever.
It is better to take refuge in the LORD
    than to trust in man.
It is better to take refuge in the LORD
    than to trust in princes.

℟. (22) The stone rejected by the builders has become the cornerstone.
*or:* ℟. Alleluia.

I will give thanks to you, for you have answered me
    and have been my savior.
The stone which the builders rejected
    has become the cornerstone.
By the LORD has this been done;
    it is wonderful in our eyes.

℟. (22) The stone rejected by the builders has become the cornerstone.
*or:* ℟. Alleluia.

Blessed is he who comes in the name of the LORD;
    we bless you from the house of the LORD.
I will give thanks to you, for you have answered me
    and have been my savior.
Give thanks to the LORD, for he is good;
    for his kindness endures forever.

℟. (22) The stone rejected by the builders has become the cornerstone.
*or:* ℟. Alleluia.

*See Appendix, p. 205, for Second Reading*

### Reflecting on Living the Gospel

In the gospel for this Sunday, Jesus proclaims that "I am the good shepherd" and "I know mine and mine know me." To know Jesus is to be one with him, the Good Shepherd. This means that we are not only sheep who hear our Good Shepherd's voice and come to know him, but we also are to become good shepherds ourselves. Transformed from sheep to shepherd, we take up the life our Good Shepherd has laid down. Jesus requires of us disciples the same mission—to also lay down our lives.

### Connecting the Responsorial Psalm to the Readings

The readings and responsorial psalm for this Sunday present us with two very different images of Christ: cornerstone and good shepherd. One is an image of rock, the other of flesh and blood, and their juxtaposition deepens our understanding of who Jesus is for us. As cornerstone he is the foundation upon whom we can build our lives. As shepherd he knows us intimately and loves us so fully that he lays down his life for us. Both images tell us we can count on Christ. There is no salvation through anyone else (first reading). He lays down his life for us on his own power (gospel). Rejection by other powers-that-be poses no ultimate threat to his mission of salvation (first reading, psalm). Christ is the one who never crumbles, the one who never flinches from the demands of saving us, the one who supports, the one who loves, the one on whom we stand, and the one whom we follow. Christ is the one for whom we give God thanks when we sing this psalm.

### Psalmist Preparation

As you prepare to sing this responsorial psalm, you might reflect on questions such as these: How is Christ the foundation of your life? How is Christ the Good Shepherd leading and supporting you? How is Christ faithful to you at all costs? How do you give Christ thanks?

### Prayer

Loving God, you have given us your risen Son as the cornerstone of our lives and the shepherd of our ways. Help us stand upright and walk confidently with him as we journey down the road of discipleship to the fullness of life. We ask this through him, our Brother and Savior. Amen.

### Gospel (John 15:1-8; L53B)

Jesus said to his disciples: "I am the true vine, and my Father is the vine grower. He takes away every branch in me that does not bear fruit, and every one that does he prunes so that it bears more fruit. You are already pruned because of the word that I spoke to you. Remain in me, as I remain in you. Just as a branch cannot bear fruit on its own unless it remains on the vine, so neither can you unless you remain in me. I am the vine, you are the branches. Whoever remains in me and I in him will bear much fruit, because without me you can do nothing. Anyone  who does not remain in me will be thrown out like a branch and wither; people will gather them and throw them into a fire and they will be burned. If you remain in me and my words remain in you, ask for whatever you want and it will be done for you. By this is my Father glorified, that you bear much fruit and become my disciples."

### First Reading (Acts 9:26-31)

When Saul arrived in Jerusalem he tried to join the disciples, but they were all afraid of him, not believing that he was a disciple. Then Barnabas took charge of him and brought him to the apostles, and he reported to them how he had seen the Lord, and that he had spoken to him, and how in Damascus he had spoken out boldly in the name of Jesus. He moved about freely with them in Jerusalem, and spoke out boldly in the name of the Lord. He also spoke and debated with the Hellenists, but they tried to kill him. And when the brothers learned of this, they took him down to Caesarea and sent him on his way to Tarsus.

The church throughout all Judea, Galilee, and Samaria was at peace. It was being built up and walked in the fear of the Lord, and with the consolation of the Holy Spirit it grew in numbers.

### Responsorial Psalm (Ps 22:26-27, 28, 30, 31-32)

℟. (26a) I will praise you, Lord, in the assembly of your people. *or:* ℟. Alleluia.

I will fulfill my vows before those who fear the LORD.
The lowly shall eat their fill;

they who seek the LORD shall praise him:
  "May your hearts live forever!"

R̸. I will praise you, Lord, in the assembly of your people.
*or:* R̸. Alleluia.

All the ends of the earth
  shall remember and turn to the LORD;
all the families of the nations
  shall bow down before him.

R̸. I will praise you, Lord, in the assembly of your people.
*or:* R̸. Alleluia.

To him alone shall bow down
  all who sleep in the earth;
before him shall bend
  all who go down into the dust.

R̸. I will praise you, Lord, in the assembly of your people.
*or:* R̸. Alleluia.

And to him my soul shall live;
  my descendants shall serve him.
Let the coming generation be told of the LORD
  that they may proclaim to a people yet to be born
  the justice he has shown.

R̸. I will praise you, Lord, in the assembly of your people.
*or:* R̸. Alleluia.

*See Appendix, p. 205, for Second Reading*

### Reflecting on Living the Gospel

The pruning of which Jesus speaks in this gospel is simply a means to an end. The end is the bearing of much fruit. To this end, Jesus' word has a twofold purpose. On the one hand, his word is prophetic and prunes whatever drains life out of his disciples. On the other, his word is the very sap of life that enables disciples to remain in him and bear fruit. True discipleship is to "remain" in Jesus. Only then does his risen Life bloom in us for all to see.

### Connecting the Responsorial Psalm to the Readings

An Israelite facing trouble, danger, or death typically vowed to offer God a thanksgiving sacrifice and to proclaim God's saving deeds before the world if God would intervene to save. This is the meaning of the first line of today's responsorial psalm. What is the vow we fulfill as we sing these words this Sunday? Having been saved through the life, death, and resurrection of Christ, we vow to "remain" joined to him as a branch to the vine (gospel). We fulfill this vow by believing in him, by loving one another not only in word but also in deed (second reading). We fulfill this vow by letting Jesus' words run through our being as life-giving sap, and by allowing God to do whatever pruning is necessary that we may bear fruit (gospel). By fulfilling our vow, we draw all people, those living and those dead, even those not yet born, to worship and serve the God who saves (psalm).

### Psalmist Preparation

On Palm Sunday you sang parts of Psalm 22 as a lament. On this, the Fifth Sunday of Easter, you sing verses from Psalm 22 in which the cries of abandonment have been transformed into words of praise for the God who saves. What will help you move from one way of singing this psalm to another? What "pruning" might God need to do within you for this to happen?

### Prayer

God of life, in your goodness you shape our hearts to conform more fully to your Son. Keep us attached to his life-giving grace and faithful to his word that we may bear fruit in his name for all the world to see. We ask this through him, our Brother and Savior. Amen.

### Gospel (John 15:9-17; L56B)

Jesus said to his disciples: "As the Father loves me, so I also love you. Remain in my love. If you keep my commandments, you will remain in my love, just as I have kept my Father's commandments and remain in his love.

"I have told you this so that my joy may be in you and your joy might be complete. This is my commandment: love one another as I love you. No one has greater love than this, to lay down one's life for one's friends. You are my friends if you do what I command you. I no longer call you slaves, because a slave does not know what his master is doing. I have called you friends, because I have told you everything I have heard from my Father. It was not you who chose me, but I who chose you and appointed you to go and bear fruit that will remain, so that whatever you ask the Father in my name he may give you. This I command you: love one another."

### First Reading (Acts 10:25-26, 34-35, 44-48)

When Peter entered, Cornelius met him and, falling at his feet, paid him homage. Peter, however, raised him up, saying, "Get up. I myself am also a human being."

Then Peter proceeded to speak and said, "In truth, I see that God shows no partiality. Rather, in every nation whoever fears him and acts uprightly is acceptable to him."

While Peter was still speaking these things, the Holy Spirit fell upon all who were listening to the word. The circumcised believers who had accompanied Peter were astounded that the gift of the Holy Spirit should have been poured out on the Gentiles also, for they could hear them speaking in tongues and glorifying God. Then Peter responded, "Can anyone withhold the water for baptizing these people, who have received the Holy Spirit even as we have?" He ordered them to be baptized in the name of Jesus Christ.

***Responsorial Psalm* (Ps 98:1, 2-3, 3-4)**

℟. (cf. 2b) The Lord has revealed to the nations his saving power. *or:* ℟.
Alleluia.

Sing to the LORD a new song,
　　for he has done wondrous deeds;
His right hand has won victory for him,
　　his holy arm.

℟. The Lord has revealed to the nations his saving power.
*or:* ℟. Alleluia.

The LORD has made his salvation known:
　　in the sight of the nations he has revealed his justice.
He has remembered his kindness and his faithfulness
　　toward the house of Israel.

℟. The Lord has revealed to the nations his saving power.
*or:* ℟. Alleluia.

All the ends of the earth have seen
　　the salvation by our God.
Sing joyfully to the LORD, all you lands;
　　break into song; sing praise.

℟. The Lord has revealed to the nations his saving power.
*or:* ℟. Alleluia.

*See Appendix, p. 205, for Second Reading*

### Reflecting on Living the Gospel
Immediately after Jesus expresses the desire that his joy become complete in us, he commands us to "love one another." What is his joy? The
deep resonance of risen Life that arises from being faithful to the Father's will. What is the love he commands? Laying "down one's life." Joy
and love are the Easter mystery made visible. We who remain in Jesus'
love and welcome his joy in us embody the Easter mystery, make visible
God's saving events.

### Connecting the Responsorial Psalm to the Readings
The full text of Psalm 98 uses the number seven as a literary device to
communicate the fullness of God's eschatological plan of salvation. The

psalm names God seven times, describes seven divine actions, lists seven divine attributes, and employs seven verbs of praise. The Lectionary uses verses from Psalm 98 for the Christmas Mass During the Day. By using further verses on this, the Sixth Sunday of Easter, the Lectionary is telling us that God's work of salvation begun with the birth of Jesus has come to completion in his resurrection. Already power is falling upon the Gentiles (first reading). John tells us this power is nothing less than God's love (second reading). It is now for us to tell the world (psalm refrain) by giving evidence of this divine power in our loving, joyful manner of living (gospel).

### Psalmist Preparation

In this responsorial psalm you express the joy of the church that God's saving power has been revealed to all peoples. How does your manner of living—at home, at work, on the street—reveal this joy?

### Prayer

Redeeming God, you have chosen us in love to bear the fruit of love in the world. Help us remain in your love, willing to lay down our lives for others in fidelity to the command of your Son, Jesus. We ask this through him, our Brother and Savior. Amen.

### Gospel (Mark 16:15-20; L58B)

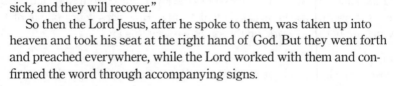

Jesus said to his disciples: "Go into the whole world and proclaim the gospel to every creature. Whoever believes and is baptized will be saved; whoever does not believe will be condemned. These signs will accompany those who believe: in my name they will drive out demons, they will speak new languages. They will pick up serpents with their hands, and if they drink any deadly thing, it will not harm them. They will lay hands on the sick, and they will recover."

So then the Lord Jesus, after he spoke to them, was taken up into heaven and took his seat at the right hand of God. But they went forth and preached everywhere, while the Lord worked with them and confirmed the word through accompanying signs.

### First Reading (Acts 1:1-11)

In the first book, Theophilus, I dealt with all that Jesus did and taught until the day he was taken up, after giving instructions through the Holy Spirit to the apostles whom he had chosen. He presented himself alive to them by many proofs after he had suffered, appearing to them during forty days and speaking about the kingdom of God. While meeting with them, he enjoined them not to depart from Jerusalem, but to wait for "the promise of the Father about which you have heard me speak; for John baptized with water, but in a few days you will be baptized with the Holy Spirit."

When they had gathered together they asked him, "Lord, are you at this time going to restore the kingdom to Israel?" He answered them, "It is not for you to know the times or seasons that the Father has established by his own authority. But you will receive power when the Holy Spirit comes upon you, and you will be my witnesses in Jerusalem, throughout Judea and Samaria, and to the ends of the earth." When he had said this, as they were looking on, he was lifted up, and a cloud took him from their sight. While they were looking intently at the sky as he was going, suddenly two men dressed in white garments stood beside them. They said, "Men of Galilee, why are you standing there looking at the sky? This Jesus who has been taken up from you into heaven will return in the same way as you have seen him going into heaven."

### Responsorial Psalm (Ps 47:2-3, 6-7, 8-9)

℟. (6) God mounts his throne to shouts of joy: a blare of trumpets for the Lord. *or:* ℟. Alleluia.

All you peoples, clap your hands,
  shout to God with cries of gladness,
for the LORD, the Most High, the awesome,
  is the great king over all the earth.

℟. God mounts his throne to shouts of joy: a blare of trumpets for the Lord. *or:* ℟. Alleluia.

God mounts his throne amid shouts of joy;
  the LORD, amid trumpet blasts.
Sing praise to God, sing praise;
  sing praise to our king, sing praise.

℟. God mounts his throne to shouts of joy: a blare of trumpets for the Lord. *or:* ℟. Alleluia.

For king of all the earth is God;
  sing hymns of praise.
God reigns over the nations,
  God sits upon his holy throne.

℟. God mounts his throne to shouts of joy: a blare of trumpets for the Lord. *or:* ℟. Alleluia.

*See Appendix, p. 206, for Second Reading*

### Reflecting on Living the Gospel

As the Jesus of history takes his leave of this world, it is clear that he intends his saving mission to continue. Seemingly without question, fear, or hesitation, the disciples "went forth." But they did not go forth alone: "the Lord worked with them." The mission, the work, and the signs are of the Lord Jesus. This relationship is the guarantee of Jesus' continued mission. So the gospel raises this question for disciples today: Are we of the Lord Jesus?

### Connecting the Responsorial Psalm to the Readings

The verses we sing from Psalm 47 for the solemnity of the Ascension are about more than the historical event of Jesus' being lifted up into the heavens. They are also a promise about our ultimate victory over sin and death. Jesus' victory will be our victory, for the one who has commissioned us to proclaim the gospel (gospel) has also promised us the power to do so (first reading). Paul reminds us that each of us has been given the grace of Christ to carry out our particular part of the mission, and this is the hope of our call (second reading). On dark days, then, when we do not know when the kingdom is to come (first reading), when we must wait patiently, remaining faithful to the daily virtues of Christian living (second reading), we can still shout, "God mounts his throne" (psalm refrain) and so do we!

### Psalmist Preparation

This responsorial psalm is not a memorial of a past event, but a celebration of a present reality. It is a declaration that the risen Christ is ascendant over sin and death, and that we, his body on earth, will complete the mission he has given us. Victory is his, and victory is ours! Spend some time this week identifying where—in your life, in the church, in the world—you have seen this victory taking place.

### Prayer

God of glory, you raised us with your Son to be seated at your right hand. With him, we are victors over sin and death. With him, we sing your praises forever. Lead us, with him, to give our lives that all peoples may know the dignity to which you have called them. We ask this through him, our Brother and Savior. Amen.

### Gospel (John 17:11b-19; L60B)

Lifting up his eyes to heaven, Jesus prayed, saying:
"Holy Father, keep them in your name that
you have given me, so that they may be one
just as we are one. When I was with them I
protected them in your name that you gave
me, and I guarded them, and none of them
was lost except the son of destruction, in
order that the Scripture might be fulfilled.
But now I am coming to you. I speak this in
the world so that they may share my joy completely. I gave them your word, and the world hated
them, because they do not belong to the world any more than I belong to
the world. I do not ask that you take them out of the world but that you
keep them from the evil one. They do not belong to the world any more
than I belong to the world. Consecrate them in the truth. Your word is
truth. As you sent me into the world, so I sent them into the world. And I
consecrate myself for them, so that they also may be consecrated in
truth."

### First Reading (Acts 1:15-17, 20a, 20c-26)

Peter stood up in the midst of the brothers—there was a group of about
one hundred and twenty persons in the one place—. He said, "My brothers, the Scripture had to be fulfilled which the Holy Spirit spoke beforehand through the mouth of David, concerning Judas, who was the guide
for those who arrested Jesus. He was numbered among us and was allotted a share in this ministry.

"For it is written in the Book of Psalms:

*May another take his office.*

"Therefore, it is necessary that one of the men who accompanied us
the whole time the Lord Jesus came and went among us, beginning from
the baptism of John until the day on which he was taken up from us, become with us a witness to his resurrection." So they proposed two, Judas
called Barsabbas, who was also known as Justus, and Matthias. Then
they prayed, "You, Lord, who know the hearts of all, show which one of
these two you have chosen to take the place in this apostolic ministry
from which Judas turned away to go to his own place." Then they gave
lots to them, and the lot fell upon Matthias, and he was counted with the
eleven apostles.

### Responsorial Psalm (Ps 103:1-2, 11-12, 19-20)

R︎. (19a) The Lord has set his throne in heaven. *or:* R︎. Alleluia.

Bless the LORD, O my soul;
   and all my being, bless his holy name.
Bless the LORD, O my soul,
   and forget not all his benefits.

R︎. (19a) The Lord has set his throne in heaven. *or:* R︎. Alleluia.

For as the heavens are high above the earth,
   so surpassing is his kindness toward those who fear him.
As far as the east is from the west,
   so far has he put our transgressions from us.

R︎. (19a) The Lord has set his throne in heaven. *or:* R︎. Alleluia.

The LORD has established his throne in heaven,
   and his kingdom rules over all.
Bless the LORD, all you his angels,
   you mighty in strength, who do his bidding.

R︎. (19a) The Lord has set his throne in heaven. *or:* R︎. Alleluia.

*See Appendix, p. 206, for Second Reading*

### Reflecting on Living the Gospel

Jesus is not naive about sending out disciples. His lengthy prayer for them (and us) recognizes that there will be resistance ("the world hated them") to the word of truth. Nevertheless, Jesus' prayer assures us that we are never alone. We are one with each other in the Body of Christ. And one with Christ, his Father, and their Spirit. In spite of the hard work of proclaiming the Gospel and meeting resistance, disciples experience joy because their relationship with God is secure.

### Connecting the Responsorial Psalm to the Readings

The second reading for this Sunday assures us of God's love: "God is love, and whoever remains in love remains in God." The responsorial psalm describes this divine love which graces our lives as a kindness and mercy higher than the heavens and wider than the universe; in other words, as a love far beyond any we can ever imagine. In the gospel Jesus asks the Father to protect us. How well he knows from personal experience the demands discipleship will make upon us, the struggles we will face with the "world," the evil we will be called upon to confront. But he also knows from personal experience how much God's love will embrace us as we pursue the mission to which he has called us. Like the early disciples we can take hold of this mission with decisiveness (first reading). We needn't hesitate, for the God who reigns in heaven (see psalm refrain) dwells in love within us (second reading).

### Psalmist Preparation

In this responsorial psalm you sing about a God enthroned in heaven whose power is made known on earth through the kindness and forgiveness he showers upon humankind. Christ sends you into the world to make God's kingdom known (gospel). How this week can you show God's kindness? How this week can you reveal God's forgiveness?

### Prayer

God of power and might, you sent your Son to reveal that you dwell not only in heaven but also in our hearts. In him we have been consecrated to your truth. Keep us faithful to this consecration and send us forth with courage and power to be his redeeming presence in the world. We ask this through him, our Brother and Savior. Amen.

**Gospel (John 15:26-27; 16:12-15; L63B)**

Jesus said to his disciples: "When the Advocate comes whom I will send you from the Father, the Spirit of truth that proceeds from the Father, he will testify to me. And you also testify, because you have been with me from the beginning.

"I have much more to tell you, but you cannot bear it now. But when he comes, the Spirit of truth, he will guide you to all truth. He will not speak on his own, but he will speak what he hears, and will declare to you the things that are coming. He will glorify me, because he will take from what is mine and declare it to you. Everything that the Father has is mine; for this reason I told you that he will take from what is mine and declare it to you."

**or Gospel (John 20:19-23; L63B)**

**First Reading (Acts 2:1-11)**

When the time for Pentecost was fulfilled, they were all in one place together. And suddenly there came from the sky a noise like a strong driving wind, and it filled the entire house in which they were. Then there appeared to them tongues as of fire, which parted and came to rest on each one of them. And they were all filled with the Holy Spirit and began to speak in different tongues, as the Spirit enabled them to proclaim.

Now there were devout Jews from every nation under heaven staying in Jerusalem. At this sound, they gathered in a large crowd, but they were confused because each one heard them speaking in his own language. They were astounded, and in amazement they asked, "Are not all these people who are speaking Galileans? Then how does each of us hear them in his native language? We are Parthians, Medes, and Elamites, inhabitants of Mesopotamia, Judea and Cappadocia, Pontus and Asia, Phrygia and Pamphylia, Egypt and the districts of Libya near Cyrene, as well as travelers from Rome, both Jews and converts to Judaism, Cretans and Arabs, yet we hear them speaking in our own tongues of the mighty acts of God."

*Responsorial Psalm* (Ps 104:1, 24, 29-30, 31, 34)

℞. (cf. 30) Lord, send out your Spirit, and renew the face of the earth.
*or:* ℞. Alleluia.

Bless the LORD, O my soul!
    O LORD, my God, you are great indeed!
How manifold are your works, O LORD!
    The earth is full of your creatures.

℞. Lord, send out your Spirit, and renew the face of the earth.
*or:* ℞. Alleluia.

If you take away their breath, they perish
    and return to their dust.
When you send forth your spirit, they are created,
    and you renew the face of the earth.

℞. Lord, send out your Spirit, and renew the face of the earth.
*or:* ℞. Alleluia.

May the glory of the LORD endure forever;
    may the LORD be glad in his works!
Pleasing to him be my theme;
    I will be glad in the LORD.

℞. Lord, send out your Spirit, and renew the face of the earth.
*or:* ℞. Alleluia.

*See Appendix, p. 206, for Second Reading*

### Reflecting on Living the Gospel
We celebrate this Sunday a wondrous and unprecedented gift of God—"the Spirit of truth" given to us. This Spirit of truth changes us—through the Spirit we share a common identity as the Body of Christ and take up a common mission to proclaim the Gospel. The Spirit propels us to engage with the world in a new way: we testify to the mighty acts of God through the very way that we live. The truth God gives transforms us and, through us, transforms the world.

### Connecting the Responsorial Psalm to the Readings

In Psalm 104 we beg God to send the Spirit of renewal upon the earth. This Spirit will enable us to receive the truth of God and give testimony to Christ. This Spirit will bear in us the fruits of "love, joy, peace, patience, kindness," and much more (second reading). The Spirit, then, renews the earth by first transforming us. Moreover, the Spirit enables us to communicate the good news of salvation in whatever tongue is necessary for people to hear and understand (first reading). What we pray for in this responsorial psalm, then, is not extraneous to our very selves. Nor is it minuscule in scope. We are asking that the Spirit re-create us, so that, through us, the Spirit may re-create the earth (psalm).

### Psalmist Preparation

As you sing the responsorial psalm for Pentecost, you celebrate the Spirit's wonderful deeds and renewing energies. But you also pray for your own transformation. The renewal of the earth begins within you. Where has the Spirit been leading you to grow in "love, joy, peace, patience, kindness, generosity, faithfulness, gentleness, [and] self-control" (second reading)? Are you willing to allow the Spirit to continue transforming you?

### Prayer

Creating God, you continually send your Spirit to renew our relationships through the power of forgiveness. Open our hearts to hear what the Spirit teaches and strengthen our wills to do as the Spirit directs, that the face of the earth may be renewed. We ask this through Christ our Lord. Amen.

### Gospel (Matt 28:16-20; L165B)

The eleven disciples went to Galilee, to the mountain to which Jesus had ordered them. When they all saw him, they worshiped, but they doubted. Then Jesus approached and said to them, "All power in heaven and on earth has been given to me. Go, therefore, and make disciples of all nations, baptizing them in the name of the Father, and of the Son, and of the Holy Spirit, teaching them to observe all that I have commanded you. And behold, I am with you always, until the end of the age."

### First Reading (Deut 4:32-34, 39-40)

Moses said to the people: "Ask now of the days of old, before your time, ever since God created man upon the earth; ask from one end of the sky to the other: Did anything so great ever happen before? Was it ever heard of? Did a people ever hear the voice of God speaking from the midst of fire, as you did, and live? Or did any god venture to go and take a nation for himself from the midst of another nation, by testings, by signs and wonders, by war, with strong hand and outstretched arm, and by great terrors, all of which the LORD, your God, did for you in Egypt before your very eyes? This is why you must now know, and fix in your heart, that the LORD is God in the heavens above and on earth below, and that there is no other. You must keep his statutes and commandments that I enjoin on you today, that you and your children after you may prosper, and that you may have long life on the land which the LORD, your God, is giving you forever."

### Responsorial Psalm (Ps 33:4-5, 6, 9, 18-19, 20, 22)

℟. (12b) Blessed the people the Lord has chosen to be his own.

Upright is the word of the LORD,
   and all his works are trustworthy.
He loves justice and right;
   of the kindness of the LORD the earth is full.

℟. Blessed the people the Lord has chosen to be his own.

By the word of the LORD the heavens were made;
    by the breath of his mouth all their host.
For he spoke, and it was made;
    he commanded, and it stood forth.

R℣. Blessed the people the Lord has chosen to be his own.

See, the eyes of the LORD are upon those who fear him,
    upon those who hope for his kindness,
To deliver them from death
    and preserve them in spite of famine.

R℣. Blessed the people the Lord has chosen to be his own.

Our soul waits for the LORD,
    who is our help and our shield.
May your kindness, O LORD, be upon us
    who have put our hope in you.

R℣. Blessed the people the Lord has chosen to be his own.

*See Appendix, p. 207, for Second Reading*

### Reflecting on Living the Gospel
In this gospel passage for the solemnity of the Most Holy Trinity, Jesus commands the disciples to baptize "in the name of the Father, and of the Son, and of the Holy Spirit." Jesus reveals his undivided, divine relationship with the Father when he declares, "All power in heaven and on earth has been given to me." Baptism professes our faith in the Holy Trinity and celebrates our insertion into the intimate, relational life of Father, Son, and Holy Spirit.

### Connecting the Responsorial Psalm to the Readings
The readings for Trinity Sunday reveal God's desire to relate to human beings with unimaginable intimacy. God takes Israel as "a nation for himself" (first reading). God adopts us as children (second reading). Jesus promises us his personal presence "until the end" (gospel). God chooses us human beings to participate in the intimate personal relationship which is the very core of the divine nature. "Did anything so great ever happen before?" (first reading). The mystery of the Trinity may be beyond our comprehension, but the desire of the Trinity's heart has been revealed to us continually throughout salvation history. The Trinity loves us and has chosen us as its own (psalm refrain). Blessed are we!

### Psalmist Preparation

As you sing this responsorial psalm refrain remember that you yourself have been chosen to be God's own. How does this awareness affect your sense of yourself? Remember also that God desires to draw all people into the embrace of the Trinity. How does this awareness affect your sense of others?

### Prayer

Three-Person God, you have chosen us as your own and drawn us into the mystery of your intimate love. May we be signs of your love and instruments of your kindness to all whom we meet so that they, too, may come to know themselves as your beloved children. We ask this through Christ our Lord. Amen.

### Gospel (Mark 14:12-16, 22-16; L168B)

On the first day of the Feast of Un-leavened Bread, when they sacri-ficed the Passover lamb, Jesus' disciples said to him, "Where do you want us to go and prepare for you to eat the Passover?" He sent two of his disciples and said to them, "Go into the city and a man will meet you, carrying a jar of water. Follow

him. Wherever he enters, say to the master of the house, 'The Teacher says, "Where is my guest room where I may eat the Passover with my disciples?"' Then he will show you a large upper room furnished and ready. Make the preparations for us there." The disciples then went off, entered the city, and found it just as he had told them; and they prepared the Passover.

While they were eating, he took bread, said the blessing, broke it, gave it to them, and said, "Take it; this is my body." Then he took a cup, gave thanks, and gave it to them, and they all drank from it. He said to them, "This is my blood of the covenant, which will be shed for many. Amen, I say to you, I shall not drink again the fruit of the vine until the day when I drink it new in the kingdom of God." Then, after singing a hymn, they went out to the Mount of Olives.

### First Reading (Exod 24:3-8)

When Moses came to the people and related all the words and ordi-nances of the LORD, they all answered with one voice, "We will do every-thing that the LORD has told us." Moses then wrote down all the words of the LORD and, rising early the next day, he erected at the foot of the mountain an altar and twelve pillars for the twelve tribes of Israel. Then, having sent certain young men of the Israelites to offer holocausts and sacrifice young bulls as peace offerings to the LORD, Moses took half of the blood and put it in large bowls; the other half he splashed on the altar. Taking the book of the covenant, he read it aloud to the people, who answered, "All that the LORD has said, we will heed and do." Then he took the blood and sprinkled it on the people, saying, "This is the blood of the covenant that the LORD has made with you in accordance with all these words of his."

*Responsorial Psalm* **(Ps 116:12-13, 15-16, 17-18)**

℟. (13) I will take the cup of salvation, and call on the name of the Lord.
*or:* ℟. Alleluia.

How shall I make a return to the LORD
   for all the good he has done for me?
The cup of salvation I will take up,
   and I will call upon the name of the LORD.

℟. I will take the cup of salvation, and call on the name of the Lord.
*or:* ℟. Alleluia.

Precious in the eyes of the LORD
   is the death of his faithful ones.
I am your servant, the son of your handmaid;
   you have loosed my bonds.

℟. I will take the cup of salvation, and call on the name of the Lord.
*or:* ℟. Alleluia.

To you will I offer sacrifice of thanksgiving,
   and I will call upon the name of the LORD.
My vows to the LORD I will pay
   in the presence of all his people.

℟. I will take the cup of salvation, and call on the name of the Lord.
*or:* ℟. Alleluia.

*See Appendix, p. 207, for Second Reading*

### Reflecting on Living the Gospel

The annual Passover meal celebrates the Jewish people "passing over" from lives of slavery and drudgery in Egypt to lives of freedom and abundance in the Promised Land. This meal portends another passover—Jesus' own passing over from suffering and death to risen Life. And yet another passover: our passing over from old self to new self, from life of sin to life of grace. Each Eucharist, each time we eat and drink the Body and Blood of Christ, we embrace anew our passing over to new Life in Christ.

# THE MOST HOLY BODY AND BLOOD OF CHRIST (CORPUS CHRISTI)

### Connecting the Responsorial Psalm to the Readings

What does it mean for us to "take the cup of salvation" (psalm refrain)? For a Hebrew this phrase meant taking a cup of wine and pouring it out as a libation in thanksgiving for some saving deed on God's part. On this solemnity we sing this refrain with added meaning. The cup of salvation that is poured out is Christ's Blood, his very life given for our salvation (second reading). We take up this cup not to pour it out, however, but to drink it (gospel) so that our blood, transformed into Christ's, may be poured out for others. The libation we make in thanksgiving for God's saving deeds in Christ is to tip over the cup of our own hearts in self-sacrificing love. How precious is such death in God's eyes (psalm)! How challenging on our part! May we sing this refrain aware of what we are saying.

### Psalmist Preparation

In these verses from Psalm 116, you thank God for the gift of redemption in Christ. You also promise to become God's faithful servant. You promise to "take [up] the cup of salvation" in the same way Christ does: as your own blood to be poured out for others. Where in your life at this moment are you being called to pour out your blood? How will God help you?

### Prayer

Redeeming God, the death of those who, like Jesus, give their lives for the sake of others is truly precious to you. May we who drink his blood poured out for us freely pour out our blood for others. May you give us the courage and strength we need to do so. We ask this through him, our Brother and Savior. Amen.

**JUNE 14, 2015**

### Gospel (Mark 4:26-34; L92B)

Jesus said to the crowds: "This is how it is with the kingdom of God; it is as if a man were to scatter seed on the land and would sleep and rise night and day and through it all the seed would sprout and grow, he knows not how. Of its own accord the land yields fruit, first the blade, then the ear, then the full grain in the ear. And when the grain is ripe, he wields the sickle at once, for the harvest has come."

He said, "To what shall we compare the kingdom of God, or what parable can we use for it? It is like a mustard seed that, when it is sown in the ground, is the smallest of all the seeds on the earth. But once it is sown, it springs up and becomes the largest of plants and puts forth large branches, so that the birds of the sky can dwell in its shade." With many such parables he spoke the word to them as they were able to understand it. Without parables he did not speak to them, but to his own disciples he explained everything in private.

### First Reading (Ezek 17:22-24)

Thus says the Lord God:

I, too, will take from the crest of the cedar,
    from its topmost branches tear off a tender shoot,
and plant it on a high and lofty mountain;
    on the mountain heights of Israel I will plant it.
It shall put forth branches and bear fruit,
    and become a majestic cedar.
Birds of every kind shall dwell beneath it,
    every winged thing in the shade of its boughs.
And all the trees of the field shall know
    that I, the Lord,
bring low the high tree,
    lift high the lowly tree,
wither up the green tree,
    and make the withered tree bloom.
As I, the Lord, have spoken, so will I do.

### Responsorial Psalm (Ps 92:2-3, 13-14, 15-16)

R̺. (cf. 2a) Lord, it is good to give thanks to you.

It is good to give thanks to the LORD,
　　to sing praise to your name, Most High,
to proclaim your kindness at dawn
　　and your faithfulness throughout the night.

R̺. Lord, it is good to give thanks to you.

The just one shall flourish like the palm tree,
　　like a cedar of Lebanon shall he grow.
They that are planted in the house of the LORD
　　shall flourish in the courts of our God.

R̺. Lord, it is good to give thanks to you.

They shall bear fruit even in old age;
　　vigorous and sturdy shall they be,
declaring how just is the LORD,
　　my rock, in whom there is no wrong.

R̺. Lord, it is good to give thanks to you.

### Reflecting on Living the Gospel

In this gospel both the land and the mustard seed actualize their potential—they do what by nature they are created to do. The "kingdom of God" is visible when we, like the land and mustard seed, actualize our own potential and do what we are called to do as Jesus' disciples. What are we to do? Hear God's word, nurture it in the fertile soil of our hearts, and let it sprout good works. In this way we become living parables doing what God created us to do.

### Connecting the Responsorial Psalm to the Readings

The first reading reminds us it is not our efforts which assure salvation, but God's. The context of the reading is the destruction of Israel by Babylon. Into their despair Ezekiel speaks words of hope: God will take from this destroyed people "a tender shoot" and will replant it "on the mountain heights of Israel." Nothing will stop God from doing this.

Jesus tells us that because of God's steadfast and attentive care even the smallest seed becomes a large plant (gospel). Such growth occurs without our intervention, while we sleep (gospel), because God has designed things so. The good news for us is that we are the tender shoots transplanted by God, the seed scattered by God for silent growth, the trees planted in the house of the Lord to "bear fruit even in old age" (psalm). The kingdom of God will come to fruition in us and in the world. We have God's very Self on whom to hang this hope. Let us give God thanks!

### Psalmist Preparation

In the midst of destruction and despair, God replants the tender shoot of life (first reading). In the silent hours of our nighttime sleep, God pursues the growth of the kingdom (gospel). What seeds of growth is God planting in you? What tender shoots is God nurturing? How this week can you thank God for this?

### Prayer

Redeeming God, you plant us within your dwelling place and guard our growth from youth to old age. May we come to full maturity in Christ and bear the fruit for which you have planted and nourished us. We ask this through him, our Brother and Savior. Amen.

### Gospel (Mark 4:35-41; L95B)

On that day, as evening drew on, Jesus said to his
disciples: "Let us cross to the other side." Leaving the crowd, they took Jesus with them in the
boat just as he was. And other boats were with
him. A violent squall came up and waves were
breaking over the boat, so that it was already
filling up. Jesus was in the stern, asleep on a
cushion. They woke him and said to him,
"Teacher, do you not care that we are perishing?" He woke up, rebuked the wind, and
said to the sea, "Quiet! Be still!" The wind
ceased and there was great calm. Then he
asked them, "Why are you terrified? Do you not
yet have faith?" They were filled with great awe
and said to one another, "Who then is this whom
even wind and sea obey?"

### First Reading (Job 38:1, 8-11)

The Lord addressed Job out of the storm and said:
Who shut within doors the sea,
    when it burst forth from the womb;
when I made the clouds its garment
    and thick darkness its swaddling bands?
When I set limits for it
    and fastened the bar of its door,
and said: Thus far shall you come but no farther,
    and here shall your proud waves be stilled!

### Responsorial Psalm (Ps 107:23-24, 25-26, 28-29, 30-31)

R̸. (1b) Give thanks to the Lord, his love is everlasting.
*or:* R̸. Alleluia.

They who sailed the sea in ships,
    trading on the deep waters,
these saw the works of the LORD
    and his wonders in the abyss.

R̸. Give thanks to the Lord, his love is everlasting.
*or:* R̸. Alleluia.

His command raised up a storm wind
    which tossed its waves on high.
They mounted up to heaven; they sank to the depths;
    their hearts melted away in their plight.

R℣. Give thanks to the Lord, his love is everlasting.
*or:* R℣. Alleluia.

They cried to the LORD in their distress;
    from their straits he rescued them,
he hushed the storm to a gentle breeze,
    and the billows of the sea were stilled.

R℣. Give thanks to the Lord, his love is everlasting.
*or:* R℣. Alleluia.

They rejoiced that they were calmed,
    and he brought them to their desired haven.
Let them give thanks to the LORD for his kindness
    and his wondrous deeds to the children of men.

R℣. Give thanks to the Lord, his love is everlasting.
*or:* R℣. Alleluia.

### Reflecting on Living the Gospel

At the end of a day of preaching and healing, Jesus was no doubt tired. The disciples took him in the boat "just as he was." So, Jesus fell fast asleep. When a "violent squall" arose, the disciples thought that Jesus didn't care that they were "perishing." But Jesus did care; he came precisely to save humanity from perishing. The disciples' faith is weak because the disciples do not yet know who Jesus is and why he came. We, however, do. So how strong is *our* faith?

### Connecting the Responsorial Psalm to the Readings

Psalm 107 as a whole relates the story of God's continual intervention to save Israel from distress and terror. The psalm conveys these terrors through vivid images of thirst experienced in the desert, fear felt in face of primordial darkness, agony suffered because of fatal illness, and perils undergone on the sea. In every situation Israel called upon God and was saved.

    The verses we sing today invite us to have the same faith in God as did Israel. When dangers and disasters mark our journey of discipleship we needn't be surprised or terrified. Such traumas are inevitable, but so is the intervention of the One whom wind and sea obey (first reading, gospel). The psalm assures us that our all-powerful God will calm not only these "storms" but also our overwhelmed hearts, for God's saving love is steadfast and everlasting (refrain).

### Psalmist Preparation

It is important that you not let the concrete imagery of this responsorial psalm sidetrack you from its real meaning. The storm is but a metaphor: you are not singing about dangers at sea but about the ongoing reality of faithful discipleship. How does this metaphor shed light on your own experience of discipleship? How does it strengthen your trust in the God who saves?

### Prayer

All-powerful God, you sent your Son to reveal your power over all that endangers our faith in your loving care of us. Keep us strong in faith that we may remain courageous in discipleship. We ask this in his name. Amen.

**JUNE 28, 2015**

### Gospel (Mark 5:21-43 [or Mark 5:21-24, 35b-43]; L98B)

[When Jesus had crossed again in the boat to the other side, a large crowd gathered around him, and he stayed close to the sea. One of the synagogue officials, named Jairus, came forward. Seeing him he fell at his feet and pleaded earnestly with him, saying, "My daughter is at the point of death. Please, come lay your hands on her that she may get well and live." He went off with him, and a large crowd followed him and pressed upon him.]

There was a woman afflicted with hemorrhages for twelve years. She had suffered greatly at the hands of many doctors and had spent all that she had. Yet she was not helped but only grew worse. She had heard about Jesus and came up behind him in the crowd and touched his cloak. She said, "If I but touch his clothes, I shall be cured." Immediately her flow of blood dried up. She felt in her body that she was healed of her affliction. Jesus, aware at once that power had gone out from him, turned around in the crowd and asked, "Who has touched my clothes?" But his disciples said to Jesus, "You see how the crowd is pressing upon you, and yet you ask, 'Who touched me?'" And he looked around to see who had done it. The woman, realizing what had happened to her, approached in fear and trembling. She fell down before Jesus and told him the whole truth. He said to her, "Daughter, your faith has saved you. Go in peace and be cured of your affliction."

[While he was still speaking, people from the synagogue official's house arrived and said, "Your daughter has died; why trouble the teacher any longer?" Disregarding the message that was reported, Jesus said to the synagogue official, "Do not be afraid; just have faith." He did not allow anyone to accompany him inside except Peter, James, and John, the brother of James. When they arrived at the house of the synagogue official, he caught sight of a commotion, people weeping and wailing loudly. So he went in and said to them, "Why this commotion and weeping? The child is not dead but asleep." And they ridiculed him. Then he put them all out. He took along the child's father and mother and those who were with him and entered the room where the child was. He took the child by the hand and said to her, *"Talitha koum,"* which means, "Little girl, I say to you, arise!" The girl, a child of twelve, arose immediately and walked around. At that they were utterly astounded. He gave strict orders that no one should know this and said that she should be given something to eat.]

### First Reading (Wis 1:13-15; 2:23-24)

God did not make death,
    nor does he rejoice in the destruction of the living.
For he fashioned all things that they might have being;
    and the creatures of the world are wholesome,
and there is not a destructive drug among them
    nor any domain of the netherworld on earth,
    for justice is undying.
For God formed man to be imperishable;
    the image of his own nature he made him.
But by the envy of the devil, death entered the world,
    and they who belong to his company experience it.

### Responsorial Psalm (Ps 30:2, 4, 5-6, 11, 12, 13)

R∕. (2a) I will praise you, Lord, for you have rescued me.

I will extol you, O Lord, for you drew me clear
    and did not let my enemies rejoice over me.
O Lord, you brought me up from the netherworld;
    you preserved me from among those going down into
        the pit.

R∕. I will praise you, Lord, for you have rescued me.

Sing praise to the Lord, you his faithful ones,
    and give thanks to his holy name.
For his anger lasts but a moment;
    a lifetime, his good will.
At nightfall, weeping enters in,
    but with the dawn, rejoicing.

R∕. I will praise you, Lord, for you have rescued me.

Hear, O Lord, and have pity on me;
    O Lord, be my helper.
You changed my mourning into dancing;
    O Lord, my God, forever will I give you thanks.

R∕. I will praise you, Lord, for you have rescued me.

### Reflecting on Living the Gospel

Faith in who Jesus is and what he can do brings us to act. Jairus approaches Jesus directly, kneels before him, and asks for healing for his daughter. The "woman afflicted with hemorrhages" dares not approach Jesus directly; she simply wishes to "touch his clothes" to be cured. In both cases their faith gave them the courage to approach Jesus and raised their expectation that he had the power to heal. Our faith, too, gives us courage and expectation. What do we do with it?

### Connecting the Responsorial Psalm to the Readings

The Sunday Lectionary uses Psalm 30 four times (Easter Vigil 4, Third Sunday of Easter C, Tenth Sunday in Ordinary Time C, and Thirteenth Sunday in Ordinary Time B) and each time the readings deal with our need to be delivered from death. Even though God has made all things for life (first reading), we nonetheless experience death coming toward us over and over, in many guises. We find ourselves caught in the middle of a cosmic struggle between the force of life and the force of death. The good news, as the gospel so concretely dramatizes, is that Christ holds the ultimate power in this struggle. By singing these verses from Psalm 30 we acknowledge what oftentimes only our faith can see: that death with its contingent weeping and mourning is not the end of the story— life is. It is no wonder that we can sing with such confidence.

### Psalmist Preparation

When you sing this psalm you embody the confidence of the entire Body of Christ that God saves from death, even when the whole world groans under its threat. Pray this week for those who are facing death in any form—physical, mental, emotional. Pray that you become a vessel of hope for them.

### Prayer

God of life, you bring all that exists into being and sustain life in every form. As the reality of death confronts us may the promise of new life granted us in Jesus turn our mourning into dancing and our grieving into joy. We ask this through him, our Brother and Savior. Amen.

### Gospel (Mark 6:1-6; L101B)

Jesus departed from there and came to his native place, accompanied by his disciples. When the sabbath came he began to teach in the synagogue, and many who heard him were astonished. They said, "Where did this man get all this? What kind of wisdom has been given him? What mighty deeds are wrought by his hands! Is he not the carpenter, the son of Mary, and the brother of James and Joses and Judas and Simon? And are not his sisters here with us?" And they took offense at him. Jesus said to them, "A prophet is not without honor except in his native place and among his own kin and in his own house." So he was not able to perform any mighty deed there, apart from curing a few sick people by laying his hands on them. He was amazed at their lack of faith.

### First Reading (Ezek 2:2-5)

As the LORD spoke to me, the spirit entered into me and set me on my feet, and I heard the one who was speaking say to me: Son of man, I am sending you to the Israelites, rebels who have rebelled against me; they and their ancestors have revolted against me to this very day. Hard of face and obstinate of heart are they to whom I am sending you. But you shall say to them: Thus says the Lord GOD! And whether they heed or resist—for they are a rebellious house—they shall know that a prophet has been among them.

### Responsorial Psalm (Ps 123:1-2, 2, 3-4)

R̂. (2cd) Our eyes are fixed on the Lord, pleading for his mercy.

To you I lift up my eyes
    who are enthroned in heaven—
As the eyes of servants
    are on the hands of their masters.

R̂. Our eyes are fixed on the Lord, pleading for his mercy.

As the eyes of a maid
    are on the hands of her mistress,

So are our eyes on the L ORD, our God,
 till he have pity on us.

℞. Our eyes are fixed on the Lord, pleading for his mercy.

Have pity on us, O L ORD, have pity on us,
 for we are more than sated with contempt;
our souls are more than sated
 with the mockery of the arrogant,
 with the contempt of the proud.

℞. Our eyes are fixed on the Lord, pleading for his mercy.

### Reflecting on Living the Gospel

The limited expectations of those in Jesus' "native place" blocked their ability to see in faith who Jesus really was. In response to Jesus' teaching and wisdom, mighty deeds and healings, "they took offense." Their limited expectations limited Jesus' own ability to show that a new in-breaking of God was among them. This gospel challenges us to examine the limits of our own expectations about who Jesus is and what he can do for us.

### Connecting the Responsorial Psalm to the Readings

What is the mercy for which we plead in this responsorial psalm refrain? Are we prophets like Jesus and Ezekiel who need God's support to remain faithful to our mission despite intense opposition from those closest to us (gospel, first reading)? Or are we the ones who reject the words of Jesus because we refuse to recognize who he is (gospel)? Chances are, the answer is sometimes one and sometimes the other. The good news is that in either case God hears our cry for mercy and responds. Because of God's response, we can do whatever is necessary, be it to remain faithful servants of God (psalm), or to open our eyes to see Jesus more clearly. We have only to fix our eyes in the right direction (psalm refrain).

### Psalmist Preparation

Whether you speak the word of God or hear that word spoken by another, you need to keep your eyes fixed firmly on God. Only by doing this can you be faithful to your mission as psalmist. What helps you remain faithful? What helps you keep your eyes focused on God?

*Prayer*

Gracious God, we are your faithful servants who keep our gaze upon you
and your holy will. Show us what you would have us do and guide us
with your love to carry it out. We ask this through Christ our Lord.
Amen.

### Gospel (Mark 6:7-13; L104B)

Jesus summoned the Twelve and began to send them out two by two and gave them authority over unclean spirits. He instructed them to take nothing for the journey but a walking stick—no food, no sack, no money in their belts. They were, however, to wear sandals but not a second tunic. He said to them, "Wherever you enter a house, stay there until you leave. Whatever place does not welcome you or listen to you, leave there and shake the dust off your feet in testimony against them." So they went off and preached repentance. The Twelve drove out many demons, and they anointed with oil many who were sick and cured them.

### First Reading (Amos 7:12-15)

Amaziah, priest of Bethel, said to Amos, "Off with you, visionary, flee to the land of Judah! There earn your bread by prophesying, but never again prophesy in Bethel; for it is the king's sanctuary and a royal temple." Amos answered Amaziah, "I was no prophet, nor have I belonged to a company of prophets; I was a shepherd and a dresser of sycamores. The LORD took me from following the flock, and said to me, Go, prophesy to my people Israel."

### Responsorial Psalm (Ps 85:9-10, 11-12, 13-14)

R℣. (8) Lord, let us see your kindness, and grant us your salvation.

I will hear what God proclaims;
    the LORD—for he proclaims peace.
Near indeed is his salvation to those who fear him,
    glory dwelling in our land.

R℣. Lord, let us see your kindness, and grant us your salvation.

Kindness and truth shall meet;
    justice and peace shall kiss.
Truth shall spring out of the earth,
    and justice shall look down from heaven.

R℣. Lord, let us see your kindness, and grant us your salvation.

The LORD himself will give his benefits;
  our land shall yield its increase.
Justice shall walk before him,
  and prepare the way of his steps.

℟. Lord, let us see your kindness, and grant us your salvation.

### Reflecting on Living the Gospel

"Jesus *summoned* the Twelve." "Summoned" is a significant word here. This is a call that cannot be ignored because the mission is so urgent: to preach repentance. The mission is so urgent that the Twelve are not even to burden themselves with seeming necessities of life. The mission is so urgent that the Twelve are given Jesus' own authority to expel demons and cure illnesses. The mission is so urgent that we ourselves must respond faithfully as did the Twelve.

### Connecting the Responsorial Psalm to the Readings

God sent Amos on a mission to prophesy to "the people Israel" (first reading). Jesus sent the Twelve on a mission to preach repentance (gospel). Neither Amos nor the Twelve chose this mission. The call to be prophet, the mission to preach and the power to confront evil and cure disease come not from ourselves but from God. In these verses from Psalm 85, we pray to hear and see what we are to preach and do. We promise to hear God proclaiming peace, and see God bringing together kindness and truth, justice and peace. We also announce the good news that despite the opposition and rejection we will face (first reading and gospel), God will bring the mission to completion. We can count on it.

### Psalmist Preparation

Do you hear what God is proclaiming in the world? Do you see what God is doing? How does your singing of this responsorial psalm proclaim that you do, indeed, hear and see what God is doing for human salvation? How does your daily living proclaim it?

### Prayer

Redeeming God, you call us to be prophets who announce your truth and disciples who do your healing works. May we remain faithful to this mission so that all the world may see your kindness and know your salvation. We ask this through Christ our Lord. Amen.

**JULY 19, 2015**

### Gospel (Mark 6:30-34; L107B)

The apostles gathered together with Jesus and reported all they had done and taught. He said to them, "Come away by yourselves to a deserted place and rest a while." People were coming and going in great numbers, and they had no opportunity even to eat. So they went off in the boat by themselves to a deserted place. People saw them leaving and many came to know about it. They hastened there on foot from all the towns and arrived at the place before them.

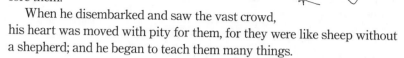

When he disembarked and saw the vast crowd, his heart was moved with pity for them, for they were like sheep without a shepherd; and he began to teach them many things.

### First Reading (Jer 23:1-6)

Woe to the shepherds who mislead and scatter the flock of my pasture, says the LORD. Therefore, thus says the LORD, the God of Israel, against the shepherds who shepherd my people: You have scattered my sheep and driven them away. You have not cared for them, but I will take care to punish your evil deeds. I myself will gather the remnant of my flock from all the lands to which I have driven them and bring them back to their meadow; there they shall increase and multiply. I will appoint shepherds for them who will shepherd them so that they need no longer fear and tremble; and none shall be missing, says the LORD.

Behold, the days are coming, says the LORD,
    when I will raise up a righteous shoot to David;
as king he shall reign and govern wisely,
    he shall do what is just and right in the land.
In his days Judah shall be saved,
    Israel shall dwell in security.
This is the name they give him:
    "The LORD our justice."

**Responsorial Psalm (Ps 23:1-3, 3-4, 5, 6)**

R̸. (1) The Lord is my shepherd; there is nothing I shall want.

The LORD is my shepherd; I shall not want.
  In verdant pastures he gives me repose;
beside restful waters he leads me;
  he refreshes my soul.

R̸. The Lord is my shepherd; there is nothing I shall want.

He guides me in right paths
  for his name's sake.
Even though I walk in the dark valley
  I fear no evil; for you are at my side
with your rod and your staff
  that give me courage.

R̸. The Lord is my shepherd; there is nothing I shall want.

You spread the table before me
  in the sight of my foes;
you anoint my head with oil;
  my cup overflows.

R̸. The Lord is my shepherd; there is nothing I shall want.

Only goodness and kindness follow me
  all the days of my life;
and I shall dwell in the house of the LORD
  for years to come.

R̸. The Lord is my shepherd; there is nothing I shall want.

## Reflecting on Living the Gospel

Jesus, the true shepherd of God, always responds to the needs of others. How does Jesus respond when the apostles return from their mission and report to him? He invites them to come away and rest. How does Jesus respond when the crowd persists in hastening to him? He teaches them. In fact, he shepherds both the apostles and the crowd. Jesus shepherds everyone toward fuller life through both the re-creating power of rest and the transforming possibilities of new teaching.

### Connecting the Responsorial Psalm to the Readings

Psalm 23, perhaps the best known and most loved of all the psalms, uses two images for God: shepherd and host. Both images communicate how God cares for, protects, nurtures, and feeds us. In Jeremiah when the appointed leaders fail to care, God intervenes and promises to send new shepherds (first reading). In the gospel when the disciples are exhausted and the crowd lost and leaderless, Jesus responds to both groups with care and compassion. Jesus reveals himself to be the new shepherd promised by God.

We might ask as we sing this psalm whether we are the crowd in need of care and direction or the disciples in need of rest. If we look deeply enough we will see that the answer is "both" and that Jesus pays heed to us in either case. May we rest in him from the labors of discipleship; may we learn from him all that we need for salvation.

### Psalmist Preparation

According to Psalm 23, God will leave you wanting for nothing. Do you believe this? Do you tell God your wants and needs? What is it that you want? What is it that you need?

### Prayer

Shepherd God, you watch over our path and lead us to fullness of life at your banquet table. Trusting in your watchful care, may we walk the journey of discipleship with courage and confidence. We ask this through Christ our Lord. Amen.

### Gospel (John 6:1-15; L110B)

Jesus went across the Sea of Galilee. A large crowd followed him, because they saw the signs he was performing on the sick. Jesus went up on the mountain, and there he sat down with his disciples. The Jewish feast of Passover was near. When Jesus raised his eyes and saw that a large crowd was coming to him, he said to Philip, "Where can we  buy enough food for them to eat?" He said this to test him, because he himself knew what he was going to do. Philip answered him, "Two hundred days' wages worth of food would not be enough for each of them to have a little." One of his disciples, Andrew, the brother of Simon Peter, said to him, "There is a boy here who has five barley loaves and two fish; but what good are these for so many?" Jesus said, "Have the people recline." Now there was a great deal of grass in that place. So the men reclined, about five thousand in number. Then Jesus took the loaves, gave thanks, and distributed them to those who were reclining, and also as much of the fish as they wanted. When they had had their fill, he said to his disciples, "Gather the fragments left over, so that nothing will be wasted." So they collected them, and filled twelve wicker baskets with fragments from the five barley loaves that had been more than they could eat. When the people saw the sign he had done, they said, "This is truly the Prophet, the one who is to come into the world." Since Jesus knew that they were going to come and carry him off to make him king, he withdrew again to the mountain alone.

### First Reading (2 Kings 4:42-44)

A man came from Baal-shalishah bringing to Elisha, the man of God, twenty barley loaves made from the firstfruits, and fresh grain in the ear. Elisha said, "Give it to the people to eat." But his servant objected, "How can I set this before a hundred people?" Elisha insisted, "Give it to the people to eat. For thus says the LORD, 'They shall eat and there shall be some left over.'" And when they had eaten, there was some left over, as the LORD had said.

### Responsorial Psalm (Ps 145:10-11, 15-16, 17-18)

R̸. (cf. 16) The hand of the Lord feeds us; he answers all our needs.

Let all your works give you thanks, O LORD,
 and let your faithful ones bless you.
Let them discourse of the glory of your kingdom
 and speak of your might.

R̸. The hand of the Lord feeds us; he answers all our needs.

The eyes of all look hopefully to you,
 and you give them their food in due season;
you open your hand
 and satisfy the desire of every living thing.

R̸. The hand of the Lord feeds us; he answers all our needs.

The LORD is just in all his ways
 and holy in all his works.
The LORD is near to all who call upon him,
 to all who call upon him in truth.

R̸. The hand of the Lord feeds us; he answers all our needs.

### Reflecting on Living the Gospel

Let's let a miracle be a miracle! Jesus tested Philip, who failed the test because he fixated on calculating the amount of food needed to feed the
hungry crowd and its cost. Jesus "knew what he was going to do"—he
gave the crowd "as much . . . as they wanted." Amazingly, the miracle
of giving them "as much . . . as they wanted" was still less than the
other miracle Jesus gave them: "the sign" of the fullness of messianic
Life. So much Life—even "twelve wicker baskets" more than they
wanted.

### Connecting the Responsorial Psalm to the Readings

Elisha feeds a hundred people with "twenty barley loaves" and has
"some left over" (first reading). Jesus feeds five thousand with "five barley loaves and two fish," and has twelve baskets left over (gospel). In
Jesus, God's gift of abundant, overflowing, everlasting Life comes to fulfillment. In him every human need will be met (see psalm refrain), not
only for the twelve tribes of Israel, but for all nations.

What we need and what Jesus gives us, however, is more than bread. What we need and what Jesus gives us is Bread that will never diminish, his very self given for our salvation. In Jesus, God satisfies "the desire of every living thing" (psalm) for fullness of Life. It is this we believe, and this for which we "look hopefully" (psalm).

### Psalmist Preparation

This responsorial psalm promises that God will feed all who hunger. What human beings truly hunger for, however, is not passing satisfactions, but messianic Life which lasts forever. This is the gift God gives in the person of Jesus (gospel). How do you "look hopefully" for this Gift? Where do you find it?

### Prayer

Loving God, you satisfy our every need with more than we in our dreams can imagine. Help us discern what our deepest desires truly are and keep us turned hopefully toward you for their fulfillment. We ask this through Christ our Lord. Amen.

### Gospel (John 6:24-35; L113B)

When the crowd saw that neither Jesus nor his disciples were there, they themselves got into boats and came to Capernaum looking for Jesus. And when they found him across the sea they said to him, "Rabbi, when did you get here?" Jesus answered them and said, "Amen, amen, I say to you, you are looking for me not because you saw signs but because you ate the loaves and were filled. Do not work for food that perishes but for the food that endures for eternal life, which the Son of Man will give you. For on him the Father, God, has set his seal." So they said to him, "What can we do to accomplish the works of God?" Jesus answered and said to

them, "This is the work of God, that you believe in the one he sent." So they said to him, "What sign can you do, that we may see and believe in you? What can you do? Our ancestors ate manna in the desert, as it is written:

*He gave them bread from heaven to eat.*"

So Jesus said to them, "Amen, amen, I say to you, it was not Moses who gave the bread from heaven; my Father gives you the true bread from heaven. For the bread of God is that which comes down from heaven and gives life to the world."

So they said to him, "Sir, give us this bread always." Jesus said to them, "I am the bread of life; whoever comes to me will never hunger, and whoever believes in me will never thirst."

### First Reading (Exod 16:2-4, 12-15)

The whole Israelite community grumbled against Moses and Aaron. The Israelites said to them, "Would that we had died at the LORD's hand in the land of Egypt, as we sat by our fleshpots and ate our fill of bread! But you had to lead us into this desert to make the whole community die of famine!"

Then the LORD said to Moses, "I will now rain down bread from heaven for you. Each day the people are to go out and gather their daily portion; thus will I test them, to see whether they follow my instructions or not.

"I have heard the grumbling of the Israelites. Tell them: In the evening twilight you shall eat flesh, and in the morning you shall have your fill of bread, so that you may know that I, the LORD, am your God."

In the evening quail came up and covered the camp. In the morning a dew lay all about the camp, and when the dew evaporated, there on the surface of the desert were fine flakes like hoarfrost on the ground. On seeing it, the Israelites asked one another, "What is this?" for they did not know what it was. But Moses told them, "This is the bread that the LORD has given you to eat."

### Responsorial Psalm (Ps 78:3-4, 23-24, 25, 54)

R︎. (24b) The Lord gave them bread from heaven.

What we have heard and know,
    and what our fathers have declared to us,
we will declare to the generation to come
    the glorious deeds of the LORD and his strength
    and the wonders that he wrought.

R︎. The Lord gave them bread from heaven.

He commanded the skies above
    and opened the doors of heaven;
he rained manna upon them for food
    and gave them heavenly bread.

R︎. The Lord gave them bread from heaven.

Man ate the bread of angels,
    food he sent them in abundance.
And he brought them to his holy land,
    to the mountains his right hand had won.

R︎. The Lord gave them bread from heaven.

### Reflecting on Living the Gospel

The bread the crowd seeks is perishable. They eat this bread but become hungry again. The bread Jesus offers is eternal. Those who eat this bread will never hunger again. They cannot procure this bread because it is the Father's gift: the "true bread from heaven" that is Jesus himself. There is a tension—a grave misunderstanding—between what the crowd seeks and what Jesus offers. What do we seek? Do we seek only nourishment? Or do we seek the Bread only God can give—Bread that is abundant and Life-giving?

### Connecting the Responsorial Psalm to the Readings

Psalm 78 retells the history of God's continual interventions to save Israel, and Israel's constant failure to remember what God has done for them and remain faithful. The psalmist reminds the people this is their story and calls them to be faithful. The verses we sing this Sunday tell of God providing manna to support the Israelites on their desert journey. The first strophe sings about passing on the story of God's "glorious deeds" to generations yet to come. The third strophe sings about the end of the journey when God delivered the people to the "holy land" prepared for them.

The Lectionary uses these verses from Psalm 78 to remind us that this story is also ours. God continually acts to save us. Like the Israelites we can see and believe or we can grumble (first reading). God sends us Jesus, the Bread of Life, to nourish us on our journey into eternal life (gospel). Will we eat and be faithful, or eat and forget? The responsorial psalm challenges us to eat, remember, and remain faithful.

### Psalmist Preparation

The bread from heaven you sing about in this psalm is the person of Jesus given to us so that we may have fullness of life. In your singing you call the community to believe in this gift and remain faithful to the relationship it establishes. How is Jesus giving you bread from heaven every day? How do you remain faithful?

### Prayer

Redeeming God, you feed us with bread from heaven, the very Body of Christ given for our salvation. May we eat this bread with understanding, share this bread with love, and be this bread for all who hunger for fullness of life. We ask this through Christ our Lord. Amen.

### Gospel (John 6:41-51; L116B)

The Jews murmured about Jesus because he said, "I am the bread that came down from heaven," and they said, "Is this not Jesus, the son of Joseph? Do we not know his father and mother? Then how can he say, 'I have come down from heaven'?" Jesus answered and said to them, "Stop murmuring among yourselves. No one can come to me unless the Father who sent me draw him, and I will raise him on the last day. It is written in the prophets:

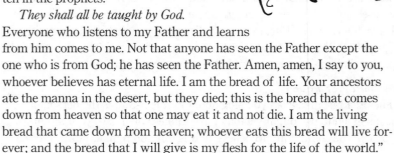

*They shall all be taught by God.*

Everyone who listens to my Father and learns from him comes to me. Not that anyone has seen the Father except the one who is from God; he has seen the Father. Amen, amen, I say to you, whoever believes has eternal life. I am the bread of life. Your ancestors ate the manna in the desert, but they died; this is the bread that comes down from heaven so that one may eat it and not die. I am the living bread that came down from heaven; whoever eats this bread will live forever; and the bread that I will give is my flesh for the life of the world."

### First Reading (1 Kings 19:4-8)

Elijah went a day's journey into the desert, until he came to a broom tree and sat beneath it. He prayed for death, saying: "This is enough, O LORD! Take my life, for I am no better than my fathers." He lay down and fell asleep under the broom tree, but then an angel touched him and ordered him to get up and eat. Elijah looked and there at his head was a hearth cake and a jug of water. After he ate and drank, he lay down again, but the angel of the LORD came back a second time, touched him, and ordered, "Get up and eat, else the journey will be too long for you!" He got up, ate, and drank; then strengthened by that food, he walked forty days and forty nights to the mountain of God, Horeb.

### Responsorial Psalm (Ps 34:2-3, 4-5, 6-7, 8-9)

R̸. (9a) Taste and see the goodness of the Lord.

I will bless the LORD at all times;
   his praise shall be ever in my mouth.
Let my soul glory in the LORD;
   the lowly will hear me and be glad.

℞. Taste and see the goodness of the Lord.

Glorify the LORD with me,
  let us together extol his name.
I sought the LORD, and he answered me
  and delivered me from all my fears.

℞. Taste and see the goodness of the Lord.

Look to him that you may be radiant with joy,
  and your faces may not blush with shame.
When the afflicted man called out, the LORD heard,
  and from all his distress he saved him.

℞. Taste and see the goodness of the Lord.

The angel of the LORD encamps
  around those who fear him and delivers them.
Taste and see how good the LORD is;
  blessed the man who takes refuge in him.

℞. Taste and see the goodness of the Lord.

### Reflecting on Living the Gospel

"The Jews murmured" because they could not get beyond their limited perception of who they thought Jesus was to the mystery about himself he reveals: "I am the bread of life," the Bread "come down from heaven," the Bread to whom we must come, the Bread who gives us a share in his "eternal life," the Bread in whom we must believe, the Bread who gives Self "for the life of the world." Jesus persists in revealing himself as the Bread sent by God to nourish the crowd (and us) for the journey to eternal Life.

### Connecting the Responsorial Psalm to the Readings

In the beginning of the first reading, Elijah is resistant to God. He is tired of life and wants to die. Even after his first feeding by an angel, he wants only to continue sleeping. But God will not leave him to either his despair or his exhaustion. God sends more food to strengthen Elijah so that he may complete his walk to the mountain.

The food God sent was not just physical bread, however. What God sent was the grace to believe and respond. In the gospel reading Jesus tells his challengers that those who have "learned from" the Father will know whom they are encountering when they meet Jesus. Those who have "tasted and seen the goodness of the Lord" (psalm) will recognize Jesus and come to him. They will hunger for what they have acquired a taste. As we sing this responsorial psalm, may those who have already been fed by God hunger for more and come gladly to receive the More which is offered.

### Psalmist Preparation

In every verse of this responsorial psalm you address the assembly. You sing about your experience of God's goodness and invite them to respond to God with your confidence and joy. Who in your life has led you to "taste and see" God's goodness? What leads you to hunger for more?

### Prayer

Gracious God, we taste and see your goodness in Jesus, the Bread of Life come down from heaven. May we praise you always for this Nourishment that leads us to eternal life. We ask this through him, our Brother and Savior. Amen.

### Gospel (Luke 1:39-56; L622)

Mary set out and traveled to the hill country in haste to a town of Judah, where she entered the house of Zechariah and greeted Elizabeth. When Elizabeth heard Mary's greeting, the infant leaped in her womb, and Elizabeth, filled with the Holy Spirit, cried out in a loud voice and said, "Blessed are you among women, and blessed is the fruit of your womb. And how does this happen to me,

that the mother of my Lord should come to me? For at the moment the sound of your greeting reached my ears, the infant in my womb leaped for joy. Blessed are you who believed that what was spoken to you by the Lord would be fulfilled."

And Mary said:

"My soul proclaims the greatness of the Lord;
my spirit rejoices in God my Savior
for he has looked upon his lowly servant.
From this day all generations will call me blessed:
the Almighty has done great things for me,
and holy is his Name.
He has mercy on those who fear him
in every generation.
He has shown the strength of his arm,
and has scattered the proud in their conceit.
He has cast down the mighty from their thrones,
and has lifted up the lowly.
He has filled the hungry with good things,
and the rich he has sent away empty.
He has come to the help of his servant Israel
for he has remembered his promise of mercy,
the promise he made to our fathers,
to Abraham and his children forever."

Mary remained with her about three months and then returned to her home.

### First Reading (Rev 11:19a; 12:1-6a, 10ab)

God's temple in heaven was opened, and the ark of his covenant could be seen in the temple.

A great sign appeared in the sky, a woman clothed with the sun, with the moon beneath her feet, and on her head a crown of twelve stars. She was with child and wailed aloud in pain as she labored to give birth. Then another sign appeared in the sky; it was a huge red dragon, with seven heads and ten horns, and on its heads were seven diadems. Its tail swept away a third of the stars in the sky and hurled them down to the earth. Then the dragon stood before the woman about to give birth, to devour her child when she gave birth. She gave birth to a son, a male child, destined to rule all the nations with an iron rod. Her child was caught up to God and his throne. The woman herself fled into the desert where she had a place prepared by God.

Then I heard a loud voice in heaven say:

"Now have salvation and power come,
and the Kingdom of our God
and the authority of his Anointed One."

### Responsorial Psalm (Ps 45:10, 11, 12, 16)

R⁊. (10bc) The queen stands at your right hand, arrayed in gold.

The queen takes her place at your right hand in gold of Ophir.

R⁊. The queen stands at your right hand, arrayed in gold.

Hear, O daughter, and see; turn your ear,
forget your people and your father's house.

R⁊. The queen stands at your right hand, arrayed in gold.

So shall the king desire your beauty;
for he is your lord.

R⁊. The queen stands at your right hand, arrayed in gold.

They are borne in with gladness and joy;
they enter the palace of the king.

R⁊. The queen stands at your right hand, arrayed in gold.

*See Appendix, p. 207 for Second Reading*

### Reflecting on Living the Gospel

"Mary set out." Her journey extended far beyond traveling to Elizabeth to help her in her need. Her journey's duration was actually Mary's life-long journey of praising God, of allowing God to do great things through her, of being an instrument for God to keep the divine promise of salvation. This day we celebrate the completion of Mary's journey, when she "returned to her home," being taken body and soul into heaven to be forever with her Lord whom she bore in her womb.

### Connecting the Responsorial Psalm to the Readings

Psalm 45 was a nuptial psalm used in the wedding ceremony between an Israelite king and his bride. The people called upon the bride to forget her family and homeland and embrace a new and more glorious relation-ship. She chose to do so, but not alone: with "gladness and joy" an entire retinue followed her.

By accepting her role in the incarnation, Mary chose to embody the cosmic struggle between the forces of evil and the saving power of God (first reading). Blessed is she for believing in the power and promise of God even when these seemed hidden from view (gospel). Blessed is she for not clinging to past and present and venturing in hope into an unseen future. Now the victory of Christ over sin and death is completed in her (second reading) and God celebrates her beauty (psalm). In her, the lowly have been lifted up and the hungering satisfied (gospel). In her, humanity has been wedded to God. And we belong to the retinue.

### Psalmist Preparation

As you sing this responsorial psalm, you celebrate your own entrance into heaven, for the entire church is borne with Mary into God's king-dom. How can you prepare yourself to sing such promise and glory? How can you imitate Mary more fully in her choice to cooperate with God's plan for salvation?

### Prayer

Glorious God, the victory of your Son over sin and death has been com-pleted in Mary whom you raised body and soul to heaven. May we, like her, always say *yes* to your holy will that one day we may share in her glory. We ask this through Christ our Lord. Amen.

### Gospel (John 6:51-58; L119B)

Jesus said to the crowds: "I am the living bread that came down from heaven; whoever eats this bread will live forever; and the bread that I will give is my flesh for the life of the world."

The Jews quarreled among themselves, saying, "How can this man give us his flesh to eat?" Jesus said to them, "Amen, amen, I say to you, unless you eat the flesh of the Son of Man and drink his blood, you do not have life within you. Whoever eats my flesh and drinks my blood has eternal life, and I will raise him on the last day. For my flesh is true food, and my blood is true drink. Whoever eats my flesh and drinks my blood remains in me and I in him. Just as the living Father sent me and I have life because of the Father, so also the one who feeds on me will have life because of me. This is the bread that came down from heaven. Unlike your ancestors who ate and still died, whoever eats this bread will live forever."

### First Reading (Prov 9:1-6)

Wisdom has built her house,
    she has set up her seven columns;
She has dressed her meat, mixed her wine,
    yes, she has spread her table.
She has sent out her maidens; she calls
    from the heights out over the city:
"Let whoever is simple turn in here";
    to the one who lacks understanding, she says,
"Come, eat of my food,
    and drink of the wine I have mixed!
Forsake foolishness that you may live;
    advance in the way of understanding."

### Responsorial Psalm (Ps 34:2-3, 4-5, 6-7)

R⍣. (9a) Taste and see the goodness of the Lord.

I will bless the LORD at all times;
    his praise shall be ever in my mouth.
Let my soul glory in the LORD;
    the lowly will hear me and be glad.

R⍣. Taste and see the goodness of the Lord.

Glorify the Lord with me,
   let us together extol his name.
I sought the Lord, and he answered me
   and delivered me from all my fears.

R∕. Taste and see the goodness of the Lord.

Look to him that you may be radiant with joy,
   and your faces may not blush with shame.
When the poor one called out, the Lord heard,
   and from all his distress he saved him.

R∕. Taste and see the goodness of the Lord.

### Reflecting on Living the Gospel

Who is "this man"? Jesus declares that he is "living bread" sent by his
"living Father"; he shares divine Life with the Father. When we eat his
flesh and drink his blood, we partake in this same divine Life. And so,
like the risen Christ, we will be the Presence of God incarnated in human
flesh. What a mystery! Its depth challenges us no less than the Jews of
Jesus' time. We, too, are faced with the question, Who is "this man"?

### Connecting the Responsorial Psalm to the Readings

Many who hear Jesus proclaim himself the Bread of Life reject what he
is saying (gospel). They simply cannot understand such radical revelation. Nor can we if we merely put our heads to it. Belief does not come
from rational explanation, however. Rather, as the words from Wisdom
and from Psalm 34 reveal, belief comes through experience. All we need
to do is simply "come and eat" (first reading), "taste and see" (psalm).

   The Lectionary repeats the psalm used last Sunday and will do so
again next week. In her wisdom the church knows that what we need to
believe is to experience over and over the life-giving nourishment that is
Jesus. The more we taste of Jesus the more we will know who he is. And
so, let us "Taste and see" that we may come to know!

### Psalmist Preparation

As you prepare to call others in this responsorial psalm to feast on the
goodness of God, you might take some time to reflect on who first called
you to the table of the Lord. Who calls you now to keep coming? Who
witnesses for you that feasting again and again on the Body and Blood
of Christ will transform your life?

## Prayer

God of goodness, you give us the Body and Blood of your Son as the food of eternal life. As we feast on this gift may our faces shine with joy and our hearts overflow with gratitude. We ask this through him, our Brother and Savior. Amen.

**AUGUST 23, 2015**

### Gospel (John 6:6:60-69; L122B)

Many of Jesus' disciples who were listening said, "This saying is hard; who can accept it?" Since Jesus knew that his disciples were murmuring about this, he said to them, "Does this shock you? What if you were to see the Son of Man ascending to where he was before? It is the spirit that gives life, while the flesh is of no avail. The words I have spoken to you are Spirit and life. But there are some of you who do not believe." Jesus knew from the beginning the ones who would
not believe and the one who would betray him. And he said, "For this reason I have told you that no one can come to me unless it is granted him by my Father."

As a result of this, many of his disciples returned to their former way of life and no longer accompanied him. Jesus then said to the Twelve, "Do you also want to leave?" Simon Peter answered him, "Master, to whom shall we go? You have the words of eternal life. We have come to believe and are convinced that you are the Holy One of God."

### First Reading (Josh 24:1-2a, 15-17, 18b)

Joshua gathered together all the tribes of Israel at Shechem, summoning their elders, their leaders, their judges, and their officers. When they stood in ranks before God, Joshua addressed all the people: "If it does not please you to serve the LORD, decide today whom you will serve, the gods your fathers served beyond the River or the gods of the Amorites in whose country you are now dwelling. As for me and my household, we will serve the LORD."

But the people answered, "Far be it from us to forsake the LORD for the service of other gods. For it was the LORD, our God, who brought us and our fathers up out of the land of Egypt, out of a state of slavery. He performed those great miracles before our very eyes and protected us along our entire journey and among the peoples through whom we passed. Therefore we also will serve the LORD, for he is our God."

# TWENTY-FIRST SUNDAY IN ORDINARY TIME

### Responsorial Psalm (Ps 34:2-3, 16-17, 18-19, 20-21)

℟. (9a) Taste and see the goodness of the Lord.

I will bless the LORD at all times;
  his praise shall be ever in my mouth.
Let my soul glory in the LORD;
  the lowly will hear me and be glad.

℟. Taste and see the goodness of the Lord.

The LORD has eyes for the just,
  and ears for their cry.
The LORD confronts the evildoers,
  to destroy remembrance of them from the earth.

℟. Taste and see the goodness of the Lord.

When the just cry out, the LORD hears them,
  and from all their distress he rescues them.
The LORD is close to the brokenhearted;
  and those who are crushed in spirit he saves.

℟. Taste and see the goodness of the Lord.

Many are the troubles of the just one,
  but out of them all the LORD delivers him;
he watches over all his bones;
  not one of them shall be broken.

℟. Taste and see the goodness of the Lord.

### Reflecting on Living the Gospel
The choice Jesus sets before the disciples in this gospel is deeper than simply "Do you also want to leave?" Jesus is inviting them to come to believe in who he is ("the Holy One of God" given as Bread from heaven) and what he offers (his own Body and Blood for eternal Life). Believing must become the lived conviction of choosing to stay with and in the risen Christ. Choosing to stay with Jesus is a way of living modeled on Jesus' own way of self-giving love.

### Connecting the Responsorial Psalm to the Readings
For the third Sunday in a row we sing, "Taste and see the goodness of the Lord" (psalm refrain). In the context of this week's first reading and gospel, however, we see that to taste and see the goodness of God requires a choice and that this choice will affect the entire direction of our

lives. While all the Israelites confronted by Joshua chose to maintain their allegiance to God, many of Jesus' disciples walked away from him, unable to believe. This Sunday's readings ask us to make our choice. Will we, like Peter, profess that we have tasted the Lord and found him good? Will we allow what we have tasted to transform us and our way of living?

### Psalmist Preparation

The Lectionary gives you the opportunity this week to really mean what you say: for the third time you sing, "Taste and see the goodness of the Lord." To whom do you sing this? For whom do you sing it? How does your way of living offer those you encounter a taste of the goodness of God?

### Prayer

Loving God, we taste and see your goodness in the gift of Jesus' Body and Blood given for our food. Increase our faith in the Eucharist that we may feed more fully on his Presence and follow more fully in his footsteps. We ask this through him, our Brother and Savior. Amen.

### Gospel (Mark 7:1-8, 14-15, 21-23; L125B)

When the Pharisees with some scribes who had come from Jerusalem gathered around Jesus, they observed that some of his disciples ate their meals with unclean, that is, unwashed, hands.—For the Pharisees and, in fact, all Jews, do not eat without carefully washing their hands, keeping the tradition of the elders. And on coming from the marketplace they do not eat without purifying themselves. And there are  many other things that they have traditionally observed, the purification of cups and jugs and kettles and beds.—So the Pharisees and scribes questioned him, "Why do your disciples not follow the tradition of the elders but instead eat a meal with unclean hands?" He responded, "Well did Isaiah prophesy about you hypocrites, as it is written:

*This people honors me with their lips,*
*but their hearts are far from me;*
*in vain do they worship me,*
*teaching as doctrines human precepts.*

You disregard God's commandment but cling to human tradition."

He summoned the crowd again and said to them, "Hear me, all of you, and understand. Nothing that enters one from outside can defile that person; but the things that come out from within are what defile.

"From within people, from their hearts, come evil thoughts, unchastity, theft, murder, adultery, greed, malice, deceit, licentiousness, envy, blasphemy, arrogance, folly. All these evils come from within and they defile."

### First Reading (Deut 4:1-2, 6-8)

Moses said to the people: "Now, Israel, hear the statutes and decrees which I am teaching you to observe, that you may live, and may enter in and take possession of the land which the LORD, the God of your fathers, is giving you. In your observance of the commandments of the LORD, your God, which I enjoin upon you, you shall not add to what I command you nor subtract from it. Observe them carefully, for thus will you give evidence of your wisdom and intelligence to the nations, who will hear of all these statutes and say, 'This great nation is truly a wise and intelligent people.' For what great nation is there that has gods so close to it as the LORD, our God, is to us whenever we call upon him? Or what great nation has statutes and decrees that are as just as this whole law which I am setting before you today?"

### Responsorial Psalm (Ps 15:2-3, 3-4, 4-5)

℟. (1a) The one who does justice will live in the presence of the Lord.

Whoever walks blamelessly and does justice;
   who thinks the truth in his heart
   and slanders not with his tongue.

℟. The one who does justice will live in the presence of the Lord.

Who harms not his fellow man,
   nor takes up a reproach against his neighbor;
by whom the reprobate is despised,
   while he honors those who fear the LORD.

℟. The one who does justice will live in the presence of the Lord.

Who lends not his money at usury
   and accepts no bribe against the innocent.
Whoever does these things
   shall never be disturbed.

℟. The one who does justice will live in the presence of the Lord.

### Reflecting on Living the Gospel

In the gospel it appears that "the Pharisees with some scribes" are judging Jesus and his disciples for how they fail to keep the Jewish traditions. In fact, Jesus is passing judgment on the Pharisees and scribes by facing them with their own self-righteousness. The Pharisees fixate on keeping human traditions; Jesus frees people from rigid adherence to human traditions. At stake is right covenantal relationship with God and others in the community. Law is about right relationships, not about self-righteousness.

### Connecting the Responsorial Psalm to the Readings

Psalm 15 was a liturgical psalm used when the Israelites ritually renewed their covenant with God. The psalm began by asking, "Lord, who may abide in your tent?" then answered by describing a person who treats others with justice. The mark of fidelity to the covenant, then, was acting justly toward one's neighbor.

In the first reading Moses commands the people to be faithful to all the statutes and decrees given them by God because the Law was a sign of God's closeness to them and was a guide to justice. When the Pharisees and scribes confront Jesus about the failure of his disciples to keep the ritual laws of washing before eating, they are not concerned with either closeness to God or justice but with undermining the authority of Jesus (gospel). Jesus responds by challenging their infidelity and calling them to the deep conversion of heart which is at the core of the Law. Psalm 15 invites us to listen to the words of Jesus by taking God's Law to heart and living lives of justice and truth. In singing it we are choosing to be persons near to our God (first reading) and near to our neighbor.

### Psalmist Preparation

This psalm challenges you by making the manner of your relating to other human beings the benchmark of your fidelity to God. Do you act with the truth, justice, and love described in the psalm? When do you struggle to act this way? When do you find it easy? How does Christ help you?

### Prayer

God of the covenant, you have made us your people and called us to treat one another with justice and truth. May we remain faithful to this call and walk always in your presence. We ask this through Christ our Lord. Amen.

**SEPTEMBER 6, 2015**

### Gospel (Mark 7:31-37; L128B)

Again Jesus left the district of Tyre and went by way of Sidon to the Sea of Galilee, into the district of the Decapolis. And people brought to him a deaf man who had a speech impediment and begged him to lay his hand on him. He took him off by himself away from the crowd. He put his finger into the man's ears and, spitting, touched his tongue; then he looked up to heaven and groaned, and said to him, *"Ephphatha!"*—that is, "Be opened!"—And immediately the man's ears were opened, his speech impediment was removed, and he spoke plainly. He ordered them not to tell anyone. But the more he ordered them not to, the more they proclaimed it. They were exceedingly astonished and they said, "He has done all things well. He makes the deaf hear and the mute speak."

### First Reading (Isa 35:4-7a)

Thus says the LORD:
Say to those whose hearts are frightened:
    Be strong, fear not!
Here is your God,
    he comes with vindication;
With divine recompense
    he comes to save you.
Then will the eyes of the blind be
      opened,

    the ears of the deaf be cleared;
Then will the lame leap like a
      stag,
    then the tongue of the mute will sing.
Streams will burst forth in the desert,
    and rivers in the steppe.
The burning sands will become pools,
    and the thirsty ground, springs of water.

### Responsorial Psalm (Ps 146:7, 8-9a, 9bc-10)

℟. (1b) Praise the Lord, my soul! *or:* ℟. Alleluia.

The God of Jacob keeps faith forever,
    secures justice for the oppressed,
    gives food to the hungry.
The LORD sets captives free.

℟. Praise the Lord, my soul! *or:* ℟. Alleluia.

The LORD gives sight to the blind;
   the Lord raises up those who were bowed down.
The LORD loves the just;
   the LORD protects strangers.

R⁖. Praise the Lord, my soul! *or:* R⁖. Alleluia.

The fatherless and the widow the LORD sustains,
   but the way of the wicked he thwarts.
The LORD shall reign forever;
   your God, O Zion, through all generations. Alleluia.

R⁖. Praise the Lord, my soul! *or:* R⁖. Alleluia.

### Reflecting on Living the Gospel

In this gospel Jesus opens the ears and loosens the tongue of the deaf-mute. Both he and the crowd cannot contain themselves, but proclaim what Jesus has done. What has Jesus really done? The miracles Jesus performs reveal his own divine power, his own compassion for the human condition, his own mission. Jesus cares for each of us, cares enough to reach out and touch us! Faced with this revelation, no one can keep silent. The Word grants the power of word.

### Connecting the Responsorial Psalm to the Readings

Psalm 146 is the first of five psalms that form the conclusion to the Hebrew Psalter. These psalms shout Alleluia to God who, throughout human history, has continually saved us, transforming impairment to wholeness, injustice to right, and suffering to joy. Isaiah proclaims God's promise to do these very things (first reading). The gospel shows these promises fully realized in the person of Jesus.

   Unlike the psalmist, however, who repeatedly commands us to shout praise for God's saving deeds (psalm refrain), Jesus commands the crowd to keep quiet about the miracle they have witnessed. In these contradictory commands, both the psalmist and Jesus want the same thing—that we see beneath the physical miracles to the deeper reality of God's gift of salvation. We are called to do more than merely shout about wonder-working. We are called to recognize salvation in our midst, and to tell the world by the way we live. This is our praise, this is our Alleluia!

### Psalmist Preparation

In this psalm you proclaim the many concrete ways God grants salvation to the suffering and the downtrodden. You offer hope to all those in the midst of such intense suffering that salvation seems impossible. You praise God for sending salvation in human form: Jesus (gospel). You sing praise to God and hope to the people. How do you need to prepare yourself to proclaim this word of salvation?

### Prayer

Gracious God, you keep faith forever for those in need of salvation. May your wondrous deeds on behalf of the lowly and the poor, the downtrodden and the oppressed, lead us to praise you now and forever. We ask this through Christ our Lord. Amen.

### Gospel (Mark 8:27-35; L131B)

Jesus and his disciples set out for the villages of Caesarea Philippi. Along the way he asked his disciples, "Who do people say that I am?" They said in reply, "John the Baptist, others Elijah, still others one of the prophets." And he asked them, "But who do you say that I am?" Peter said to him in reply, "You are the Christ." Then he warned them not to tell anyone about him.

He began to teach them that the Son of Man must suffer greatly and be rejected by the elders, the chief priests, and the scribes, and be killed, and rise after three days. He spoke this openly. Then Peter took him aside and began to rebuke him. At this he turned around and, looking at his disciples, rebuked Peter and said, "Get behind me, Satan. You are thinking not as God does, but as human beings do."

He summoned the crowd with his disciples and said to them, "Whoever wishes to come after me must deny himself, take up his cross, and follow me. For whoever wishes to save his life will lose it, but whoever loses his life for my sake and that of the gospel will save it."

### First Reading (Isa 50:4c-9a)

The Lord God opens my ear that I may hear;
    and I have not rebelled,
    have not turned back.
I gave my back to those who beat me,
    my cheeks to those who plucked my beard;
My face I did not shield
    from buffets and spitting.

The Lord God is my help,
    therefore I am not disgraced;
I have set my face like flint,
    knowing that I shall not be put to shame.
He is near who upholds my right;
    if anyone wishes to oppose me,
    let us appear together.

Who disputes my right?
  Let that man confront me.
See, the Lord God is my help;
  who will prove me wrong?

### Responsorial Psalm (Ps 116:1-2, 3-4, 5-6, 8-9)

℟. (9) I will walk before the Lord, in the land of the living.
*or:* ℟. Alleluia.

I love the Lord because he has heard
  my voice in supplication,
because he has inclined his ear to me
  the day I called.

℟. I will walk before the Lord, in the land of the living.
*or:* ℟. Alleluia.

The cords of death encompassed me;
  the snares of the netherworld seized upon me;
  I fell into distress and sorrow,
And I called upon the name of the Lord,
  "O Lord, save my life!"

℟. I will walk before the Lord, in the land of the living.
*or:* ℟. Alleluia.

Gracious is the Lord and just;
  yes, our God is merciful.
The Lord keeps the little ones;
  I was brought low, and he saved me.

℟. I will walk before the Lord, in the land of the living.
*or:* ℟. Alleluia.

For he has freed my soul from death,
  my eyes from tears, my feet from stumbling.
I shall walk before the Lord
  in the land of the living.

℟. I will walk before the Lord, in the land of the living.
*or:* ℟. Alleluia.

# TWENTY-FOURTH SUNDAY IN ORDINARY TIME

### Reflecting on Living the Gospel

Jesus is called "the Christ"—Peter is called Satan. Salvation confronts human resistance. Peter had a certain image, belief, expectation of what "the Christ" was to be, to do. Suffering, rejection, and being killed had nothing to do with Peter's Christ. But they have everything to do with the Christ of God. Without a right understanding of "the Christ," we cannot, with him, rise to new Life. We take up our own cross daily because this is the way to a share in risen Life.

### Connecting the Responsorial Psalm to the Readings

Psalm 116 was a song of thanksgiving prayed by an individual while offering a sacrifice in gratitude for God's deliverance from grave danger. On this Sunday when both the first reading and gospel place the necessity of death before us, this psalm is our statement of profound confidence in God's ultimate presence and protection. The suffering servant of Isaiah faces persecution without "turn[ing] back" (first reading). Jesus begins to teach that the cost of following him is the cross (gospel). If we remain faithful to discipleship, then, we are indeed in grave danger. But we can face the danger because we know, like the psalmist, that no danger—even death—is greater than God's desire to give us life. We know that as we walk with Jesus toward death, we walk straight "before the Lord, in[to] the land of the living" (psalm refrain).

### Psalmist Preparation

To sing this psalm well you must combine confidence in God's protection with willingness to take up the cross. How in your life does the one feed the other?

### Prayer

God of the resurrection, as we take up the cross keep us steadfast in the knowledge that you will lead us through death to new life. Grant us the courage we need to lose our lives that we may gain our lives. Lead us with your Son into the land of the living. We ask this in his name. Amen.

**SEPTEMBER 20, 2015**

### Gospel (Mark 9:30-37; L134B)

Jesus and his disciples left from there and began a journey through Galilee, but he did not wish anyone to know about it. He was teaching his disciples and telling them, "The Son of Man is to be handed over to men and they will kill him, and three days after his death the Son of Man will rise." But they did not understand the saying, and they were afraid to question him.

They came to Capernaum and, once inside the house, he began to ask them, "What were you arguing about on the way?" But they remained silent. They had been discussing among themselves on the way who was the greatest. Then he sat down, called the Twelve, and said to them, "If anyone wishes to be first, he shall be the last of all and the servant of all." Taking a child, he placed it in their midst, and putting his arms around it, he said to them, "Whoever receives one child such as this in my name, receives me; and whoever receives me, receives not me but the One who sent me."

### First Reading (Wis 2:12, 17-20)

The wicked say:
Let us beset the just one, because he is obnoxious to us;
    he sets himself against our doings,
Reproaches us for transgressions of the law
    and charges us with violations of our training.
Let us see whether his words be true;
    let us find out what will happen to him.
For if the just one be the son of God, God will defend him
    and deliver him from the hand of his foes.
With revilement and torture let us put the just one to
        the test
    that we may have proof of his gentleness
    and try his patience.
Let us condemn him to a shameful death;
    for according to his own words, God will take care of him.

### Responsorial Psalm (Ps 54:3-4, 5, 6-8)

R̲̲. (6b) The Lord upholds my life.

O God, by your name save me,
    and by your might defend my cause.
O God, hear my prayer;
    hearken to the words of my mouth.

R̲̲. The Lord upholds my life.

For the haughty men have risen up against me,
    the ruthless seek my life;
    they set not God before their eyes.

R̲̲. The Lord upholds my life.

Behold, God is my helper;
    the Lord sustains my life.
Freely will I offer you sacrifice;
    I will praise your name, O LORD, for its goodness.

R̲̲. The Lord upholds my life.

### Reflecting on Living the Gospel

The scandal of this gospel is that Jesus, the leader and teacher of the disciples, will be reduced to the least when he is handed over and dies. How do the disciples react to this scandalous teaching? They argue among themselves about who is the greatest! The disciples do not understand greatest and least, first and last, servant of all. They do not understand that Jesus' own death is a call to die to self, to choose to become the greatest by being the least.

### Connecting the Responsorial Psalm to the Readings

This responsorial psalm is a cry of confidence in face of certain death. In the first reading the wicked plot "a shameful death" for one whose righteous manner of living is an affront to their unrighteous ways. In the gospel Jesus warns the disciples that this same end is in store for him. But he promises also that on the third day he will rise. Like the psalmist, Jesus knows that God will uphold his life. We, too, can bear the consequences of discipleship because we believe that even in death God will uphold us. Such confidence does not come from intellectual conviction, but from personal intimacy with God. When we sing this psalm we are not merely whistling in the dark. We are professing faith in a saving God whose very name we know (psalm).

### Psalmist Preparation

Any normal person would rather avoid the death which fidelity to discipleship makes inevitable. How can singing this psalm give you courage? How in singing it can you give other disciples courage?

### Prayer

Loving God, you uphold our life even in the face of death. Keep us courageous in meeting the demands of faithful discipleship and humble in our service to one another. We ask this through Christ our Lord. Amen.

### Gospel (Mark 9:38-43, 45, 47-48; L137B)

At that time, John said to Jesus, "Teacher, we saw someone driving out demons in your name, and we tried to prevent him because he does not follow us." Jesus replied, "Do not prevent him. There is no one who performs a mighty deed in my name who can at the same time speak ill of me. For whoever is not against us is for us. Anyone who gives you a cup of water to drink because you belong to Christ, amen, I say to you, will surely not lose his reward.

"Whoever causes one of these little ones who believe in me to sin, it would be better for him if a great millstone were put around his neck and he were thrown into the sea. If your hand causes you to sin, cut it off. It is better for you to enter into life maimed than with two hands to go into Gehenna, into the unquenchable fire. And if your foot causes you to sin, cut if off. It is better for you to enter into life crippled than with two feet to be thrown into Gehenna. And if your eye causes you to sin, pluck it out. Better for you to enter into the kingdom of God with one eye than with two eyes to be thrown into Gehenna, where 'their worm does not die, and the fire is not quenched.'"

### First Reading (Num 11:25-29)

The Lord came down in the cloud and spoke to Moses. Taking some of the spirit that was on Moses, the Lord bestowed it on the seventy elders; and as the spirit came to rest on them, they prophesied.

Now two men, one named Eldad and the other Medad, were not in the gathering but had been left in the camp. They too had been on the list, but had not gone out to the tent; yet the spirit came to rest on them also, and they prophesied in the camp. So, when a young man quickly told Moses, "Eldad and Medad are prophesying in the camp," Joshua, son of Nun, who from his youth had been Moses' aide, said, "Moses, my lord, stop them." But Moses answered him, "Are you jealous for my sake? Would that all the people of the Lord were prophets! Would that the Lord might bestow his spirit on them all!"

### Responsorial Psalm (Ps 19:8, 10, 12-13, 14)

R∕. (9a) The precepts of the Lord give joy to the heart.

The law of the LORD is perfect,
  refreshing the soul;
the decree of the LORD is trustworthy,
  giving wisdom to the simple.

R∕. The precepts of the Lord give joy to the heart.

The fear of the LORD is pure,
  enduring forever;
the ordinances of the LORD are true,
  all of them just.

R∕. The precepts of the Lord give joy to the heart.

Though your servant is careful of them,
  very diligent in keeping them,
yet who can detect failings?
  Cleanse me from my unknown faults!

R∕. The precepts of the Lord give joy to the heart.

From wanton sin especially, restrain your servant;
  let it not rule over me.
Then shall I be blameless and innocent
  of serious sin.

R∕. The precepts of the Lord give joy to the heart.

### Reflecting on Living the Gospel

Focused completely on his saving mission to bring about the kingdom of God, Jesus directly confronts human pettiness and sinfulness. He uses graphic examples to demand that disciples turn from whatever is inconsistent with acting in his name, with continuing his mission. Any behavior which causes us to sin or to lead others into sin must be cut off. Being a disciple demands radical choices about how we live and relate to others. It means being as completely focused on Jesus' saving mission as he was.

# TWENTY-SIXTH SUNDAY IN ORDINARY TIME

### Connecting the Responsorial Psalm to the Readings

The Law of the Lord brings us refreshment, wisdom, and joy (psalm). But even the most faithful adherent can fall prey to petty jealousies (first reading and gospel). And so it is not surprising in this psalm that while we praise the purity and perfection of the Law, we also ask God to protect us from the "unknown faults" and "wanton sin" which can rule our hearts. How fortunate we are to have God's Law which acts as guide and safeguard, protecting us from more dire measures we might otherwise need to take to enter the kingdom of heaven (gospel). For as Jesus points out in no uncertain terms, we must allow nothing to stand in the way of our entrance into eternal life (gospel). Thank God for the Law which keeps us on the path of what is "perfect," "trustworthy," "pure," and "true."

### Psalmist Preparation

As you prepare to sing this Sunday's responsorial psalm you might reflect on questions such as these: What does the law of God ask of you? What wisdom have you gained because of your obedience to it? What sacrifices has such obedience required? What joys have resulted?

### Prayer

Loving God, you give us the Law to guide our lives in righteousness. Keep us blameless in following its decrees that we may conform our hearts and our actions more fully to those of your Son Jesus. We ask this in his name. Amen.

## Gospel (Mark 10:2-16 [or Mark 10:2-12]; L140B)

[The Pharisees approached Jesus and asked, "Is it lawful for a husband to divorce his wife?" They were testing him. He said to them in reply, "What did Moses command you?" They replied, "Moses permitted a husband to write a bill of divorce and dismiss her." But Jesus told them, "Because of the hardness of your hearts he wrote you this commandment. But from the beginning of creation, *God made them male and female. For this reason a man shall leave his father and mother and be joined to his wife, and the two shall become one flesh.* So they are no longer two but one flesh. Therefore what God has joined together, no human being must separate." In the house the disciples again questioned Jesus about this. He said to them, "Whoever divorces his  wife and marries another commits adultery against her; and if she divorces her husband and marries another, she commits adultery."]

And people were bringing children to him that he might touch them, but the disciples rebuked them. When Jesus saw this he became indignant and said to them, "Let the children come to me; do not prevent them, for the kingdom of God belongs to such as these. Amen, I say to you, whoever does not accept the kingdom of God like a child will not enter it." Then he embraced them and blessed them, placing his hands on them.

## First Reading (Gen 2:18-24)

The LORD God said: "It is not good for the man to be alone. I will make a suitable partner for him." So the LORD God formed out of the ground various wild animals and various birds of the air, and he brought them to the man to see what he would call them; whatever the man called each of them would be its name. The man gave names to all the cattle, all the birds of the air, and all wild animals; but none proved to be the suitable partner for the man.

So the LORD God cast a deep sleep on the man, and while he was asleep, he took out one of his ribs and closed up its place with flesh. The LORD God then built up into a woman the rib that he had taken from the man. When he brought her to the man, the man said: / "This one, at last, is bone of my bones / and flesh of my flesh; / this one shall be called 'woman,' / for out of 'her man' this one has been taken." / That is why a man leaves his father and mother and clings to his wife, and the two of them become one flesh.

### Responsorial Psalm (Ps 128:1-2, 3, 4-5, 6)

R7. (cf. 5) May the Lord bless us all the days of our lives.

Blessed are you who fear the LORD,
    who walk in his ways!
For you shall eat the fruit of your handiwork;
    blessed shall you be, and favored.

R7. May the Lord bless us all the days of our lives.

Your wife shall be like a fruitful vine
    in the recesses of your home;
your children like olive plants
    around your table.

R7. May the Lord bless us all the days of our lives.

Behold, thus is the man blessed
    who fears the LORD.
The LORD bless you from Zion:
    may you see the prosperity of Jerusalem
    all the days of your life.

R7. May the Lord bless us all the days of our lives.

May you see your children's children.
    Peace be upon Israel!

R7. May the Lord bless us all the days of our lives.

### Reflecting on Living the Gospel

The longer form of this Sunday's gospel unfolds in two interrelated situations. The Pharisees approach Jesus to test him about his stance concerning marriage and divorce; the disciples rebuke the people for bringing their children to Jesus. In both situations, Jesus upholds human relationships as fundamental to embracing the kingdom of God. In both situations, faithful ones are embraced and blessed by God. In this gospel Jesus exposes the hardness of the Pharisees' hearts. This challenges us to look deep within our own hearts.

### Connecting the Responsorial Psalm to the Readings

Because of its patriarchal imagery, Psalm 128 is a difficult one for us to pray. Understanding its original purpose, however, places the psalm in a broader context than the specifics of patriarchal family structure, and sheds light on its aptness for this Sunday's Liturgy of the Word. Psalm 128 was a song of ascents, one of a sequential set (Pss 120–34) scholars believe the Israelites sang as they traveled up to Jerusalem to celebrate their major feasts. Psalm 128 was perhaps a blessing sung over the people as they began their journey back home. The psalm is about the blessings which fidelity to "walk[ing] in [God's] ways" brings. The image of the happy family projected by the psalm was the symbol par excellence of Israel's covenant relationship with God. The blessings described—fruitfulness, fulfillment, prosperity, and peace—were extended to all of Jerusalem. Thus Psalm 128 is not so much about the blessings of marriage as it is about the blessings of a way of life faithful to the ways of God. We can sing it today, then, as a prayer for one another that our relationships in the church, in our families, and in our world truly be marked by such fidelity to God and such blessings.

### Psalmist Preparation

The refrain to this responsorial psalm is a prayer of blessing over the people. Spend some time praying this week for members of your parish and for the whole church. Pray that they know the blessings of fulfillment and peace which come from walking in the ways of God. Then, as you travel to church this Sunday, consider praying the psalm as your own song of ascent.

### Prayer

God of the covenant, you call us to be persons who relate to one another with compassion, forbearance, and humility. Help us be faithful to this calling that we may be blessed by you all the days of our lives. We ask this through Christ our Lord. Amen.

### Gospel (Mark 10:17-30 [or Mark 10:17-27]; L143B)

[As Jesus was setting out on a journey, a man ran up, knelt down before him, and asked him, "Good teacher, what must I do to inherit eternal life?" Jesus answered him, "Why do you call me good? No one is good but God alone. You know the commandments: *You shall not kill; you shall not commit adultery; you shall not steal; you shall not bear false witness; you shall not defraud; honor your father and your mother.*"

He replied and said to him, "Teacher, all of these I have observed from my youth." Jesus, looking at him, loved him and said to him, "You are lacking in one thing. Go, sell what you have, and give to the poor and you will have treasure in heaven; then come, follow me." At that statement his face fell, and he went away sad, for he had many possessions.

Jesus looked around and said to his disciples, "How hard it is for those who have wealth to enter the kingdom of God!" The disciples were amazed at his words. So Jesus again said to them in reply, "Children, how hard it is to enter the kingdom of God! It is easier for a camel to pass through the eye of a needle than for one who is rich to enter the kingdom of God." They were exceedingly astonished and said among themselves, "Then who can be saved?" Jesus looked at them and said, "For human beings it is impossible, but not for God. All things are possible for God."] Peter began to say to him, "We have given up everything and followed you." Jesus said, "Amen, I say to you, there is no one who has given up house or brothers or sisters or mother or father or children or lands for my sake and for the sake of the gospel who will not receive a hundred times more now in this present age: houses and brothers and sisters and mothers and children and lands, with persecutions, and eternal life in the age to come."

### First Reading (Wis 7:7-11)

I prayed, and prudence was given me;
    I pleaded, and the spirit of wisdom came to me.
I preferred her to scepter and throne,
and deemed riches nothing in comparison with her,
    nor did I liken any priceless gem to her;
because all gold, in view of her, is a little sand,
    and before her, silver is to be accounted mire.

Beyond health and comeliness I loved her,
and I chose to have her rather than the light,
    because the splendor of her never yields to sleep.
Yet all good things together came to me in her company,
    and countless riches at her hands.

### Responsorial Psalm (Ps 90:12-13, 14-15, 16-17)

R℣. (14) Fill us with your love, O Lord, and we will sing for joy!

Teach us to number our days aright,
    that we may gain wisdom of heart.
Return, O LORD! How long?
    Have pity on your servants!

R℣. Fill us with your love, O Lord, and we will sing for joy!

Fill us at daybreak with your kindness,
    that we may shout for joy and gladness all our days.
Make us glad, for the days when you afflicted us,
    for the years when we saw evil.

R℣. Fill us with your love, O Lord, and we will sing for joy!

Let your work be seen by your servants
    and your glory by their children;
and may the gracious care of the Lord our God be ours;
    prosper the work of our hands for us!
    Prosper the work of our hands!

R℣. Fill us with your love, O Lord, and we will sing for joy!

### Reflecting on Living the Gospel

The man in the gospel must have had an inkling that keeping the commandments was not enough, or else he never would have approached Jesus with his question about how to inherit eternal Life. In spite of his faithfulness in keeping God's commandments and his being loved by Jesus, the man nevertheless had a divided heart: "he went away sad, for he had many possessions." The man needed to turn his focus from earthly life to eternal Life, from possessions to single-heartedly following Jesus. Where is our heart?

# TWENTY-EIGHTH SUNDAY IN ORDINARY TIME

### Connecting the Responsorial Psalm to the Readings

In different words, both the young man and the disciples ask the same question in this Sunday's gospel: "How can we be saved?" Jesus answers that salvation comes only through dispossessing self of all that stands in the way of making God the complete focus of one's life. The teaching is hard—the young man walks away from it and the disciples question their ability to live it.

To all who ask, God offers the wisdom to see both the reward offered (first reading, psalm, gospel) and the price required (first reading, gospel). The price is nothing less than our giving everything; the reward is nothing less than our receiving fullness of life. But we must choose to pay the price. In the psalm refrain we ask God to fill us with the divine love we need to make this choice. God granted such love to the author of the first reading, and Jesus offered it to the young man in the gospel. Today we ask for this love, and know it will be given to us.

### Psalmist Preparation

In singing this Sunday's responsorial psalm you make a dangerous request: you ask God for the "wisdom of heart" which will lead to deeper discipleship. You are, in a sense, the young man in the gospel reading. You are also the disciples who struggle with Jesus' answer. Are you willing to make the request?

### Prayer

Loving God, you grant us wisdom of heart by filling our hearts with your love. May we recognize your love as our greatest possession and give our love back to you by following and serving your Son Jesus. We ask this in his name. Amen.

**OCTOBER 18, 2015**

### Gospel (Mark 10:35-45 [or Mark 10:42-45]; L146B)

James and John, the sons of Zebedee, came to Jesus and said to him, "Teacher, we want you to do for us whatever we ask of you." He replied, "What do you wish me to do for you?" They answered him, "Grant that in your glory we may sit one at your right and the other at your left." Jesus said to them, "You do not know what you are asking. Can you drink the cup that I drink or be baptized with the baptism with which I am baptized?" They said to him, "We can." Jesus said to them, "The cup that I drink, you will drink, and with the baptism with which I am baptized, you will be baptized; but to sit at my right or at my left is not mine to give but is for those for whom it has been prepared." When the ten heard this, they became indignant at James and John. [Jesus summoned them and said to them, "You know that those who are recognized as rulers over the Gentiles lord it over them, and their great ones make their authority over them felt. But it shall not be so among you. Rather, whoever wishes to be great among you will be your servant; whoever wishes to be first among you will be the slave of all. For the Son of Man did not come to be served but to serve and to give his life as a ransom for many."]

### First Reading (Isa 53:10-11)

The LORD was pleased
    to crush him in infirmity.

If he gives his life as an offering for sin,
    he shall see his descendants in a long life,
    and the will of the LORD shall be accomplished
        through him.

Because of his affliction
    he shall see the light in fullness of days;
Through his suffering, my servant shall justify many,
    and their guilt he shall bear.

### Responsorial Psalm (Ps 33:4-5, 18-19, 20, 22)

R℣. (22) Lord, let your mercy be on us, as we place our trust in you.

Upright is the word of the LORD,
  and all his works are trustworthy.
He loves justice and right;
  of the kindness of the LORD the earth is full.

R℣. Lord, let your mercy be on us, as we place our trust in you.

See, the eyes of the LORD are upon those who fear him,
  upon those who hope for his kindness,
To deliver them from death
  and preserve them in spite of famine.

R℣. Lord, let your mercy be on us, as we place our trust in you.

Our soul waits for the LORD,
  who is our help and our shield.
May your kindness, O LORD, be upon us
  who have put our hope in you.

R℣. Lord, let your mercy be on us, as we place our trust in you.

### Reflecting on Living the Gospel

Why did the apostles follow Jesus? This gospel suggests they had re-ward on their minds: the glory of sitting at the right and left of Jesus in positions of honor. It took the apostles a long time to learn that the real reward of following Jesus would be to "drink the cup" and "be baptized" with his baptism. His baptism was his lifelong choice to do the will of the Father no matter what the cost. As Jesus' followers, we can choose no less.

### Connecting the Responsorial Psalm to the Readings

Over and over in the refrain of this responsorial psalm we beg God for mercy. On the one hand, we need God's mercy because of our persistent failure to understand the servant demands of discipleship (gospel). On the other, we need God's mercy once we have accepted these demands, for they require that we die to self (first reading, gospel). Our call as dis-ciples is to serve as Christ served to the point of laying down our lives for the sake of others. We must "drink the cup" Christ offers. While we waver in our response, hoping to gain the glory promised without pay-ing its price, God remains steadfast toward us at all times, in every situation, to the ends of the earth (psalm). God will deliver those who "drink the cup" Jesus drinks. In this we can "place our trust" (psalm refrain).

### Psalmist Preparation

In the first strophe of this responsorial psalm you tell people about the trustworthiness of God. In the second you invite them to place their hope in God who delivers from death. In the third you speak for them as you voice their surrender to God in hope and trust. How will you communicate these shifts in the psalm? How have you experienced these shifts in your own faith journey?

### Prayer

Merciful God, you know well that those who choose to be disciples of Jesus must drink of the cup of his death. You also know well that you will deliver from death those who accept the cost of discipleship. Grant us the courage we need to enter into Jesus' death that we may one day enter into his glory. We ask this in his name. Amen.

### Gospel (Mark 10:46-52; L149B)

As Jesus was leaving Jericho with his disciples and a sizable crowd, Bartimaeus, a blind man, the son of Timaeus, sat by the roadside begging. On hearing that it was Jesus of Nazareth, he began to cry out and say, "Jesus, son of David, have pity on me." And many rebuked him, telling him to be silent. But he kept calling out all the more, "Son of David, have pity on me." Jesus stopped and said, "Call him." So they called the blind man, saying to him, "Take courage; get up, Jesus is calling you." He threw aside his cloak, sprang up, and came to Jesus. Jesus said to him in reply, "What do you want me to do for you?" The blind man replied to him, "Master, I want to see." Jesus told him, "Go your way; your faith has saved you." Immediately he received his sight and followed him on the way.

### First Reading (Jer 31:7-9)

Thus says the LORD:
Shout with joy for Jacob,
    exult at the head of the nations;
    proclaim your praise and say:
The LORD has delivered his people,
    the remnant of Israel.
Behold, I will bring them back
    from the land of the north;
I will gather them from the ends of the world,
    with the blind and the lame in their midst,
the mothers and those with child;
    they shall return as an immense throng.
They departed in tears,
    but I will console them and guide them;
I will lead them to brooks of water,
    on a level road, so that none shall stumble.
For I am a father to Israel,
    Ephraim is my first-born.

### Responsorial Psalm (Ps 126:1-2ab, 2cd-3, 4-5, 6)

℞. (3) The Lord has done great things for us; we are filled with joy.

When the LORD brought back the captives of Zion,
    we were like men dreaming.
Then our mouth was filled with laughter,
    and our tongue with rejoicing.

℞. The Lord has done great things for us; we are filled with joy.

Then they said among the nations,
    "The LORD has done great things for them."
The LORD has done great things for us;
    we are glad indeed.

℞. The Lord has done great things for us; we are filled with joy.

Restore our fortunes, O LORD,
    like the torrents in the southern desert.
Those that sow in tears
    shall reap rejoicing.

℞. The Lord has done great things for us; we are filled with joy.

Although they go forth weeping,
    carrying the seed to be sown,
They shall come back rejoicing,
    carrying their sheaves.

℞. The Lord has done great things for us; we are filled with joy.

### Reflecting on Living the Gospel

The verbs describing Bartimaeus's actions in this gospel say everything about faith, encountering Jesus, and choosing to follow him. He cried out, kept calling, threw aside his cloak, sprang up and came to Jesus, stated his request, received his sight, followed Jesus. Such need, such urgency, such conviction! These verbs describe Bartimaeus's faith-in-action, his deepening relationship with Jesus. Faith is the insight and cause of action. So must it be for us.

### Connecting the Responsorial Psalm to the Readings

In the gospel, Jesus is on a journey, leaving Jericho on his way to Jerusalem. Bartimaeus is on a journey, moving from blindness to sight, from encounter with Jesus to faith, from going his own way to walking the way of Jesus. Psalm 126 depicts a dramatic moment in Israel's journey of faith toward the God who had formed them as a people. The psalm describes their return from exile in Babylon to their homeland. At first they do not see clearly. They think they are "dreaming." But faith opens their eyes to see the "great things" (psalm refrain) God is doing for them: delivering them, gathering them home, leading them to fullness of life (see first reading). Salvation is not a dream, but real.

Psalm 126 describes our faith journey as well. Like Bartimaeus, we cry out to Jesus to heal our clouded vision. Jesus responds, and we see him as salvation made real in our midst. How can we not, like Bartimaeus, follow in his footsteps?

### Psalmist Preparation

One of the "great things" God does (psalm refrain) is grant you faith to see Jesus as Savior and grace to follow him wherever he leads. Can you accept the weeping this "great thing" will bring? Do you believe this weeping will be turned into joy?

### Prayer

God of salvation, you deliver us from the captivity of our inability to see Jesus and our hesitancy to follow him. You lead us with open eyes to the reality of the cross, and from that cross to the rejoicing that comes from new and fuller life. May we exult in this great thing you do for us and come to know the joy of your salvation. We ask this through Christ our Lord. Amen.

### Gospel (Matt 5:1-12a; L667)

When Jesus saw the crowds, he went up the mountain, and after he had sat down, his disciples came to him. He began to teach them, saying:

> "Blessed are the poor in spirit,
>   for theirs is the Kingdom of heaven.
> Blessed are they who mourn,
>   for they will be comforted.
> Blessed are the meek,
>   for they will inherit the land.
> Blessed are they who hunger and thirst for
>       righteousness,
>   for they will be satisfied.
> Blessed are the merciful,
>   for they will be shown mercy.
> Blessed are the clean of heart,
>   for they will see God.
> Blessed are the peacemakers,
>   for they will be called children of God.
> Blessed are they who are persecuted for the sake of righteousness,
>   for theirs is the Kingdom of heaven.

Blessed are you when they insult you and persecute you and utter every kind of evil against you falsely because of me. Rejoice and be glad, for your reward will be great in heaven."

### First Reading (Rev 7:2-4, 9-14)

I, John, saw another angel come up from the East, holding the seal of the living God. He cried out in a loud voice to the four angels who were given power to damage the land and the sea, "Do not damage the land or the sea or the trees until we put the seal on the foreheads of the servants of our God." I heard the number of those who had been marked with the seal, one hundred and forty-four thousand marked from every tribe of the children of Israel.

After this I had a vision of a great multitude, which no one could count, from every nation, race, people, and tongue. They stood before the throne and before the Lamb, wearing white robes and holding palm branches in their hands. They cried out in a loud voice:

"Salvation comes from our God,
  who is seated on the throne,
and from the Lamb."

All the angels stood around the throne and around the elders and the
four living creatures. They prostrated themselves before the throne,
worshiped God, and exclaimed:

"Amen. Blessing and glory, wisdom and thanksgiving,
  honor, power, and might
  be to our God forever and ever. Amen."

Then one of the elders spoke up and said to me, "Who are these wearing
white robes, and where did they come from?" I said to him, "My lord, you
are the one who knows." He said to me, "These are the ones who have
survived the time of great distress; they have washed their robes and
made them white in the Blood of the Lamb."

### Responsorial Psalm (Ps 24:1bc-2, 3-4ab, 5-6)

℟. (cf. 6) Lord, this is the people that longs to see your face.

The LORD's are the earth and its fullness;
  the world and those who dwell in it.
For he founded it upon the seas
  and established it upon the rivers.

℟. Lord, this is the people that longs to see your face.

Who can ascend the mountain of the LORD?
  or who may stand in his holy place?
One whose hands are sinless, whose heart is clean,
  who desires not what is vain.

℟. Lord, this is the people that longs to see your face.

He shall receive a blessing from the LORD,
  a reward from God his savior.
Such is the race that seeks for him,
  that seeks the face of the God of Jacob.

℟. Lord, this is the people that longs to see your face.

*See Appendix, p. 207, for Second Reading*

### Reflecting on Living the Gospel

It is no accident that the Gospel of Matthew has Jesus go "up the mountain," traditionally a place associated with divine encounter, to teach the Beatitudes to his disciples. The Beatitudes reveal the very Being of God ("Blessed," holy), God's care for God's beloved people ("poor in spirit," "those who mourn," etc.), God's intent for faithful ones ("theirs is the kingdom of heaven"). The Beatitudes reveal the mind and heart of God. Those who have encountered God and lived the Beatitudes have the same mind and heart. We call them "saints."

### Connecting the Responsorial Psalm to the Readings

Psalm 24 is one of the psalms of ascent. As the Israelites traveled to Jerusalem for solemn festival they raised their eyes to the "mountain of the Lord." Upon arrival at the temple door, they were questioned, "Who can ascend [this] mountain . . . who may stand in [this] holy place?" They then responded, "One whose hands are sinless, whose heart is clean, who desires not what is vain." These are the very qualities Jesus spells out in the Beatitudes (gospel). The Israelites were faithful to the law and the covenant because they knew they were God's chosen people. We live the Beatitudes because we know we are God's children (second reading). With the Israelites, we long to see God's face (psalm refrain). With all those who faithfully pursue this longing, we reap the reward of heaven.

### Psalmist Preparation

The first psalm strophe tells of God's power, the last of God's blessings upon those who are faithful. The middle strophe describes those who are faithful. In singing this psalm you speak sometimes to God, sometimes to the people. Pray that you may speak to both with humility and love.

### Prayer

Good and gracious God, you bestow upon us great love, calling us your own children. Teach us to live always as your holy ones, faithful to your ways of blessedness. We ask this through Christ our Lord. Amen.

### Gospel (Mark 12:38-44 [or Mark 12:41-44]; L155B)

In the course of his teaching Jesus said to the crowds, "Beware of the scribes, who like to go around in long robes and accept greetings in the marketplaces, seats of honor in synagogues, and places of honor at banquets. They devour the houses of widows and, as a pretext recite lengthy prayers. They will receive a very severe condemnation."

[He sat down opposite the treasury and observed how the crowd put money into the treasury. Many rich people put in large sums. A poor widow also came and put in two small coins worth a few cents. Calling his disciples to himself, he said to them, "Amen, I say to you, this poor widow put in more than all the other contributors to the treasury. For they have all contributed from their surplus wealth, but she, from her poverty, has contributed all she had, her whole livelihood."]

### First Reading (1 Kings 17:10-16)

In those days, Elijah the prophet went to Zarephath. As he arrived at the entrance of the city, a widow was gathering sticks there; he called out to her, "Please bring me a small cupful of water to drink." She left to get it, and he called out after her, "Please bring along a bit of bread." She answered, "As the LORD, your God, lives, I have nothing baked; there is only a handful of flour in my jar and a little oil in my jug. Just now I was collecting a couple of sticks, to go in and prepare something for myself and my son; when we have eaten it, we shall die." Elijah said to her, "Do not be afraid. Go and do as you propose. But first make me a little cake and bring it to me. Then you can prepare something for yourself and your son. For the LORD, the God of Israel, says, 'The jar of flour shall not go empty, nor the jug of oil run dry, until the day when the LORD sends rain upon the earth.'" She left and did as Elijah had said. She was able to eat for a year, and he and her son as well; the jar of flour did not go empty, nor the jug of oil run dry, as the LORD had foretold through Elijah.

### Responsorial Psalm (Ps 146:7, 8-9, 9-10)

℟. (1b) Praise the Lord, my soul! *or:* ℟. Alleluia.

The LORD keeps faith forever,
    secures justice for the oppressed,
    gives food to the hungry.
The LORD sets captives free.

℟. Praise the Lord, my soul! *or:* ℟. Alleluia.

The LORD gives sight to the blind;
    the LORD raises up those who were bowed down.
The LORD loves the just;
    the LORD protects strangers.

℟. Praise the Lord, my soul! *or:* ℟. Alleluia.

The fatherless and the widow he sustains,
    but the way of the wicked he thwarts.
The LORD shall reign forever;
    your God, O Zion, through all generations. Alleluia.

℟. Praise the Lord, my soul! *or:* ℟. Alleluia.

### Reflecting on Living the Gospel

Jesus teaches the crowds to beware of the hypocrisy of the scribes who know God's word and law, yet seek places of honor and hurt those whom the law demands they protect—the widows. Jesus condemns them severely. "Calling his disciples to himself," he teaches them that they are not to do like the scribes. They are instead to do like the widow in the temple who gives all she has. True disciples give all they have, their whole livelihood—not goods, but *themselves*.

### Connecting the Responsorial Psalm to the Readings

Psalm 146 tells of how God cares without fail for those in need—the hungry, the disabled, the bowed down, the widowed. We sang these verses from Psalm 146 on the Twenty-Third Sunday in Ordinary Time when Jesus cured a deaf-mute brought to him by the crowd. This Sunday we catch a glimpse of two widows who have lost almost everything yet willingly give to God the little they have left. God rewards the first with abundant sustenance (first reading); Jesus identifies the second as the model for all discipleship (gospel). If we are to be fully committed disciples we must give all we have for the sake of the kingdom. Nothing can be held back. When we find ourselves left with nothing because of the kingdom, we needn't fear, for we will have staked our security on a God who holds nothing back in return (psalm).

### Psalmist Preparation

This responsorial psalm needs to be sung with confidence in God's providence and protection. But unless you give all that you have—your whole heart—you will never discover what God is giving you in return. What do you hold back? What would give you the courage to hand it over?

### Prayer

Loving God, you ask for the gift not of things but of our heart. Make us generous givers with hearts ready to be filled by your abundance and feet ready to walk the way of discipleship. We ask this through Christ our Lord. Amen.

**NOVEMBER 15, 2015**

### Gospel (Mark 13:24-32; L158B)

Jesus said to his disciples: "In those days after that tribulation the sun will be darkened, and the moon will not give its light, and the stars will be falling from the sky, and the powers in the heavens will be shaken.

"And then they will see 'the Son of Man coming in the clouds' with great power and glory, and then he will send out the angels and gather his elect from the four winds, from the end of the earth to the end of the sky.

"Learn a lesson from the fig tree. When its branch becomes tender and sprouts leaves, you know that summer is near. In the same way, when you see these things happening, know that he is near, at the gates. Amen, I say to you, this generation will not pass away until all these things have taken place. Heaven and earth will pass away, but my words will not pass away.

"But of that day or hour, no one knows, neither the angels in heaven, nor the Son, but only the Father."

### First Reading (Dan 12:1-3)

In those days, I, Daniel, heard this word of the LORD:
"At that time there shall arise
    Michael, the great prince,
    guardian of your people;
It shall be a time unsurpassed in distress
    since nations began until that time.
At that time your people shall escape,
    everyone who is found written in the book.

"Many of those who sleep in the dust of the earth shall awake;
    some shall live forever,
    others shall be an everlasting horror and disgrace.

"But the wise shall shine brightly
    like the splendor of the firmament,
And those who lead the many to justice
    shall be like the stars forever."

### Responsorial Psalm (Ps 16:5, 8, 9-10, 11)

R̟. (1) You are my inheritance, O Lord!

O LORD, my allotted portion and my cup,
    you it is who hold fast my lot.
I set the LORD ever before me;
    with him at my right hand I shall not be disturbed.

R̟. You are my inheritance, O Lord!

Therefore my heart is glad and my soul rejoices,
    my body, too, abides in confidence;
Because you will not abandon my soul to the netherworld,
    nor will you suffer your faithful one to undergo corruption.

R̟. You are my inheritance, O Lord!

You will show me the path to life,
    fullness of joys in your presence,
    the delights at your right hand forever.

R̟. You are my inheritance, O Lord!

### Reflecting on Living the Gospel
In this gospel Jesus teaches about the future; his words deal with cosmic events, his final coming in power to overcome darkness, and his drawing the elect into the light of his final glory. Jesus uses the image of the greening of "the fig tree" when summer is near as a sign that "he is near." Those who hear and heed his words are in the greening of their lives. For them, the future is now.

### Connecting the Responsorial Psalm to the Readings
There will come a time of tribulation and great suffering when the world as we know it will end and certainties will be shattered (first reading, gospel). But Christ assures us that this collapse of things will be no more than the announcement of his coming (gospel) when he will send his angels to gather the elect (gospel)—those who have lived by wisdom and justice (first reading)—into life everlasting. No one knows the moment of his coming (gospel) but the readings and psalm promise life-giving judgment for those who have been faithful.

The readings—as well as Jesus' life—reveal that faithful discipleship will not protect us from catastrophe, suffering, and death. Ironically it will lead us directly to them. But we have Jesus' word as our surety (gospel) and God's promise as our hope (psalm). As we continue to walk with Jesus toward Jerusalem we pray today that we maintain our focus on God who is our "path" and our "inheritance" (psalm).

### Psalmist Preparation

As you prepare to sing this responsorial psalm, ask yourself if you really believe that God is your inheritance. What hope does this give you for the future? What strength for the present?

### Prayer

Gracious God, you give us your very Self as our inheritance. When we encounter trials and sufferings along the journey of discipleship, keep us walking joyfully along your path, confident of your presence and your promise. We ask this through Christ our Lord. Amen.

### Gospel (John 18:33b-37; L161B)

Pilate said to Jesus, "Are you the King of the Jews?" Jesus answered, "Do you say this on your own or have others told you about me?" Pilate answered, "I am not a Jew, am I? Your own nation and the chief priests handed you over to me. What have you done?" Jesus answered, "My kingdom does not belong to this world. If my kingdom did belong to this world, my attendants would be fighting to keep me from being handed over to the Jews. But as it is, my kingdom is not here." So Pilate said to him, "Then you are a king?" Jesus answered, "You say I am a king. For this I was born and for this I came into the world, to testify to the truth. Everyone who belongs to the truth listens to my voice."

### First Reading (Dan 7:13-14)

As the visions during the night continued, I saw
    one like a Son of man coming,
    on the clouds of heaven;
When he reached the Ancient One
    and was presented before him,
the one like a Son of man received dominion, glory,
        and kingship;
    all peoples, nations, and languages serve him.
His dominion is an everlasting dominion
    that shall not be taken away,
    his kingship shall not be destroyed.

### Responsorial Psalm (Ps 93:1, 1-2, 5)

R︎. (1a) The Lord is king; he is robed in majesty.

The LORD is king, in splendor robed;
    robed is the LORD and girt about with strength.

R︎. The Lord is king; he is robed in majesty.

And he has made the world firm,
    not to be moved.
Your throne stands firm from of old;
    from everlasting you are, O LORD.

R︎. The Lord is king; he is robed in majesty.

Your decrees are worthy of trust indeed;
　　holiness befits your house,
　　O LORD, for length of days.

R̶/. The Lord is king; he is robed in majesty.

*See Appendix, p. 208, for Second Reading*

### Reflecting on Living the Gospel

In this conversation Pilate questions Jesus about his identity ("Are you the King of the Jews?") and about why he is on trial ("What have you done?"). What unfolds is a conversation about two very different worlds. That of Pilate and the chief priests, in which fighting, falsehood, and obstinacy predominate. That of Jesus, in which life, truth, and openness prevail. Yes, Jesus is a King—but of a kingdom different from Herod's. To which kingdom do we choose to belong?

### Connecting the Responsorial Psalm to the Readings

The whole of Psalm 93 depicts the cosmic conflict between the forces of evil and the power of God. The Hebrews pictured the world as a platform balanced on the chaotic waters of the sea. The surging waters constantly threatened to overwhelm the earth, and would have done so were it not for the stabilizing hand of God who "made the world firm, not to be moved" (psalm). There was no doubt in the minds of the Israelites that God held ultimate power over all the forces threatening their life and well-being.

We sing these verses from Psalm 93 to celebrate the victory of Christ over sin and death. Throughout the weeks of Ordinary Time we have listened to his voice and obeyed his call to discipleship. We have walked with him to Jerusalem and the cross. Today we celebrate the glory that awaits us beyond the cross. We proclaim to the world that "The Lord is King . . . robed in majesty" (psalm) and that we are his kingdom (second reading), not to be moved (psalm).

### Psalmist Preparation

The conviction with which you will sing this psalm will be directly related to the faithfulness with which you have walked this year's journey through Ordinary Time. Take time this week to thank Christ for showing you the way and for strengthening you when you felt weak and weary. Take time also to thank Christ for the many other faithful disciples who have walked with you.

### Prayer

Lord Jesus, you come in power and glory to claim the earth as your throne. We celebrate your victory over sin and death. Keep us faithful to your service until all tribes and nations enter your kingdom of holiness, peace, and joy. We ask this in your name. Amen.

# *APPENDIX*

### FIRST SUNDAY OF ADVENT, November 30, 2014
### *Second Reading* (1 Cor 1:3-9)

Brothers and sisters: Grace to you and peace from God our Father and the Lord Jesus Christ.

I give thanks to my God always on your account for the grace of God bestowed on you in Christ Jesus, that in him you were enriched in every way, with all discourse and all knowledge, as the testimony to Christ was confirmed among you, so that you are not lacking in any spiritual gift as you wait for the revelation of our Lord Jesus Christ. He will keep you firm to the end, irreproachable on the day of our Lord Jesus Christ. God is faithful, and by him you were called to fellowship with his Son, Jesus Christ our Lord.

### SECOND SUNDAY OF ADVENT, December 7, 2014
### *Second Reading* (2 Pet 3:8-14)

Do not ignore this one fact, beloved, that with the Lord one day is like a thousand years and a thousand years like one day. The Lord does not delay his promise, as some regard "delay," but he is patient with you, not wishing that any should perish but that all should come to repentance. But the day of the Lord will come like a thief, and then the heavens will pass away with a mighty roar and the elements will be dissolved by fire, and the earth and everything done on it will be found out.

Since everything is to be dissolved in this way, what sort of persons ought you to be, conducting yourselves in holiness and devotion, waiting for and hastening the coming of the day of God, because of which the heavens will be dissolved in flames and the elements melted by fire. But according to his promise we await new heavens and a new earth in which righteousness dwells. Therefore, beloved, since you await these things, be eager to be found without spot or blemish before him, at peace.

### THE IMMACULATE CONCEPTION OF THE BLESSED VIRGIN MARY, December 8, 2014
### *Second Reading* (Eph 1:3-6, 11-12)

Brothers and sisters: Blessed be the God and Father of our Lord Jesus Christ, who has blessed us in Christ with every spiritual blessing in the heavens, as he chose us in him, before the foundation of the world, to be holy and without blemish before him. In love he destined us for adoption to himself through Jesus Christ, in accord with the favor of his will, for the praise of the glory of his grace that he granted us in the beloved.

In him we were also chosen, destined in accord with the purpose of the One who accomplishes all things according to the intention of his will, so that we might exist for the praise of his glory, we who first hoped in Christ.

### THIRD SUNDAY OF ADVENT, December 14, 2014
### *Second Reading* (1 Thess 5:16-24)

Brothers and sisters: Rejoice always. Pray without ceasing. In all circumstances give thanks, for this is the will of God for you in Christ Jesus. Do not quench the Spirit. Do not despise prophetic utterances. Test everything; retain what is good. Refrain from every kind of evil.

May the God of peace make you perfectly holy and may you entirely, spirit, soul, and body, be preserved blameless for the coming of our Lord Jesus Christ. The one who calls you is faithful, and he will also accomplish it.

## FOURTH SUNDAY OF ADVENT, December 21, 2014
### Second Reading (Rom 16:25-27)
Brothers and sisters: To him who can strengthen you, according to my gospel and the proclamation of Jesus Christ, according to the revelation of the mystery kept secret for long ages but now manifested through the prophetic writings and, according to the command of the eternal God, made known to all nations to bring about the obedience of faith, to the only wise God, through Jesus Christ be glory forever and ever. Amen.

## THE NATIVITY OF THE LORD, *Vigil Mass*, December 24, 2014
### Second Reading (Acts 13:16-17, 22-25)
When Paul reached Antioch in Pisidia and entered the synagogue, he stood up, motioned with his hand, and said, "Fellow Israelites and you others who are God-fearing, listen. The God of this people Israel chose our ancestors and exalted the people during their sojourn in the land of Egypt. With uplifted arm he led them out of it. Then he removed Saul and raised up David as king; of him he testified, 'I have found David, son of Jesse, a man after my own heart; he will carry out my every wish.' From this man's descendants God, according to his promise, has brought to Israel a savior, Jesus. John heralded his coming by proclaiming a baptism of repentance to all the people of Israel; and as John was completing his course, he would say, 'What do you suppose that I am? I am not he. Behold, one is coming after me; I am not worthy to unfasten the sandals of his feet.'"

## THE NATIVITY OF THE LORD, *Mass at Midnight*, December 25, 2014
### Second Reading (Titus 2:11-14)
Beloved: The grace of God has appeared, saving all and training us to reject godless ways and worldly desires and to live temperately, justly, and devoutly in this age, as we await the blessed hope, the appearance of the glory of our great God and savior Jesus Christ, who gave himself for us to deliver us from all lawlessness and to cleanse for himself a people as his own, eager to do what is good.

## THE NATIVITY OF THE LORD, *Mass at Dawn*, December 25, 2014
### Second Reading (Titus 3:4-7)
Beloved:
When the kindness and generous love
    of God our savior appeared,
not because of any righteous deeds we had done
    but because of his mercy,
he saved us through the bath of rebirth
    and renewal by the Holy Spirit,
whom he richly poured out on us
    through Jesus Christ our savior,
so that we might be justified by his grace
    and become heirs in hope of eternal life.

## THE NATIVITY OF THE LORD, *Mass During the Day*, December 25, 2014
### Second Reading (Heb 1:1-6)

Brothers and sisters: In times past, God spoke in partial and various ways to our ancestors through the prophets; in these last days, he has spoken to us through the Son, whom he made heir of all things and through whom he created the universe,

who is the refulgence of his glory, the very imprint of his being,
 and who sustains all things by his mighty word.
When he had accomplished purification from sins,
 he took his seat at the right hand of the Majesty on high,
as far superior to the angels
 as the name he has inherited is more excellent than theirs.

For to which of the angels did God ever say:

*You are my son; this day I have begotten you?*

Or again:

*I will be a father to him, and he shall be a son to me?*

And again, when he leads the firstborn into the world, he says:

*Let all the angels of God worship him.*

## THE HOLY FAMILY OF JESUS, MARY, AND JOSEPH, December 28, 2014
### Second Reading (Heb 11:8, 11-12, 17-19)

Brothers and sisters: By faith Abraham obeyed when he was called to go out to a place that he was to receive as an inheritance; he went out, not knowing where he was to go. By faith he received power to generate, even though he was past the normal age—and Sarah herself was sterile—for he thought that the one who had made the promise was trustworthy. So it was that there came forth from one man, himself as good as dead, descendants as numerous as the stars in the sky and as countless as the sands on the seashore.

By faith Abraham, when put to the test, offered up Isaac, and he who had received the promises was ready to offer his only son, of whom it was said, "Through Isaac descendants shall bear your name." He reasoned that God was able to raise even from the dead, and he received Isaac back as a symbol.

## SOLEMNITY OF MARY, THE HOLY MOTHER OF GOD,
### January 1, 2015
### Second Reading (Gal 4:4-7)

Brothers and sisters: When the fullness of time had come, God sent his Son, born of a woman, born under the law, to ransom those under the law, so that we might receive adoption as sons. As proof that you are sons, God sent the Spirit of his Son into our hearts, crying out, "Abba, Father!" So you are no longer a slave but a son, and if a son then also an heir, through God.

## THE EPIPHANY OF THE LORD, January 4, 2015
### Second Reading (Eph 3:2-3a, 5-6)
Brothers and sisters: You have heard of the stewardship of God's grace that was given to me for your benefit, namely, that the mystery was made known to me by revelation. It was not made known to people in other generations as it has now been revealed to his holy apostles and prophets by the Spirit: that the Gentiles are coheirs, members of the same body, and copartners in the promise in Christ Jesus through the gospel.

## THE BAPTISM OF THE LORD, January 11, 2015
### Second Reading (1 John 5:1-9 [or Acts 10:34-38])
Beloved: Everyone who believes that Jesus is the Christ is begotten by God, and everyone who loves the Father loves also the one begotten by him. In this way we know that we love the children of God when we love God and obey his commandments. For the love of God is this, that we keep his commandments. And his commandments are not burdensome, for whoever is begotten by God conquers the world. And the victory that conquers the world is our faith. Who indeed is the victor over the world but the one who believes that Jesus is the Son of God?

This is the one who came through water and blood, Jesus Christ, not by water alone, but by water and blood. The Spirit is the one who testifies, and the Spirit is truth. So there are three that testify, the Spirit, the water, and the blood, and the three are of one accord. If we accept human testimony, the testimony of God is surely greater. Now the testimony of God is this, that he has testified on behalf of his Son.

## ASH WEDNESDAY, February 18, 2015
### Second Reading (2 Cor 5:20–6:2)
Brothers and sisters: We are ambassadors for Christ, as if God were appealing through us. We implore you on behalf of Christ, be reconciled to God. For our sake he made him to be sin who did not know sin, so that we might become the righteousness of God in him.

Working together, then, we appeal to you not to receive the grace of God in vain. For he says:

*In an acceptable time I heard you,*
*and on the day of salvation I helped you.*

Behold, now is a very acceptable time; behold, now is the day of salvation.

## FIRST SUNDAY OF LENT, February 22, 2015
### Second Reading (1 Pet 3:18-22)
Beloved: Christ suffered for sins once, the righteous for the sake of the unrighteous, that he might lead you to God. Put to death in the flesh, he was brought to life in the Spirit. In it he also went to preach to the spirits in prison, who had once been disobedient while God patiently waited in the days of Noah during the building of the ark, in which a few persons, eight in all, were saved through water. This prefigured baptism, which saves you now. It is not a removal of dirt from the body but an appeal to God for a clear conscience, through the resurrection of Jesus Christ, who has gone into heaven and is at the right hand of God, with angels, authorities, and powers subject to him.

### SECOND SUNDAY OF LENT, March 1, 2015
#### *Second Reading* (Rom 8:31b-34)

Brothers and sisters: If God is for us, who can be against us? He who did not spare his own Son but handed him over for us all, how will he not also give us everything else along with him?

Who will bring a charge against God's chosen ones? It is God who acquits us, who will condemn? Christ Jesus it is who died—or, rather, was raised—who also is at the right hand of God, who indeed intercedes for us.

### THIRD SUNDAY OF LENT, March 8, 2015
#### *Second Reading* (1 Cor 1:22-25)

Brothers and sisters: Jews demand signs and Greeks look for wisdom, but we proclaim Christ crucified, a stumbling block to Jews and foolishness to Gentiles, but to those who are called, Jews and Greeks alike, Christ the power of God and the wisdom of God. For the foolishness of God is wiser than human wisdom, and the weakness of God is stronger than human strength.

### FOURTH SUNDAY OF LENT, March 15, 2015
#### *Second Reading* (Eph 2:4-10)

Brothers and sisters: God, who is rich in mercy, because of the great love he had for us, even when we were dead in our transgressions, brought us to life with Christ—by grace you have been saved—, raised us up with him, and seated us with him in the heavens in Christ Jesus, that in the ages to come he might show the immeasurable riches of his grace in his kindness to us in Christ Jesus. For by grace you have been saved through faith, and this is not from you; it is the gift of God; it is not from works, so no one may boast. For we are his handiwork, created in Christ Jesus for the good works that God has prepared in advance, that we should live in them.

### FIFTH SUNDAY OF LENT, March 22, 2015
#### *Second Reading* (Heb 5:7-9)

In the days when Christ Jesus was in the flesh, he offered prayers and supplications with loud cries and tears to the one who was able to save him from death, and he was heard because of his reverence. Son though he was, he learned obedience from what he suffered; and when he was made perfect, he became the source of eternal salvation for all who obey him.

### PALM SUNDAY OF THE LORD'S PASSION, March 29, 2015
#### *Second Reading* (Phil 2:6-11)

Christ Jesus, though he was in the form of God,
   did not regard equality with God
   something to be grasped.
Rather, he emptied himself,
   taking the form of a slave,
   coming in human likeness;
   and found human in appearance,
   he humbled himself,
   becoming obedient to the point of death,
   even death on a cross.

Because of this, God greatly exalted him
and bestowed on him the name
which is above every name,
that at the name of Jesus
every knee should bend,
of those in heaven and on earth and under the earth,
and every tongue confess that
Jesus Christ is Lord,
to the glory of God the Father.

## HOLY THURSDAY EVENING MASS OF THE LORD'S SUPPER, April 2, 2015
### Second Reading (1 Cor 11:23-26)

Brothers and sisters: I received from the Lord what I also handed on to you, that the Lord Jesus, on the night he was handed over, took bread, and, after he had given thanks, broke it and said, "This is my body that is for you. Do this in remembrance of me." In the same way also the cup, after supper, saying, "This cup is the new covenant in my blood. Do this, as often as you drink it, in remembrance of me." For as often as you eat this bread and drink the cup, you proclaim the death of the Lord until he comes.

## FRIDAY OF THE LORD'S PASSION (Good Friday), April 3, 2015
### Second Reading (Heb 4:14-16; 5:7-9)

Brothers and sisters: Since we have a great high priest who has passed through the heavens, Jesus, the Son of God, let us hold fast to our confession. For we do not have a high priest who is unable to sympathize with our weaknesses, but one who has similarly been tested in every way, yet without sin. So let us confidently approach the throne of grace to receive mercy and to find grace for timely help.

In the days when Christ was in the flesh, he offered prayers and supplications with loud cries and tears to the one who was able to save him from death, and he was heard because of his reverence. Son though he was, he learned obedience from what he suffered; and when he was made perfect, he became the source of eternal salvation for all who obey him.

## EASTER SUNDAY OF THE RESURRECTION, April 5, 2015
### Second Reading (1 Cor 5:6b-8 [or Col 3:1-4])

Brothers and sisters: Do you not know that a little yeast leavens all the dough? Clear out the old yeast, so that you may become a fresh batch of dough, inasmuch as you are unleavened. For our paschal lamb, Christ, has been sacrificed. Therefore, let us celebrate the feast, not with the old yeast, the yeast of malice and wickedness, but with the unleavened bread of sincerity and truth.

## SECOND SUNDAY OF EASTER (Divine Mercy Sunday), April 12, 2015
### Second Reading (1 John 5:1-6)

Beloved: Everyone who believes that Jesus is the Christ is begotten by God, and everyone who loves the Father loves also the one begotten by him. In this way we know that we love the children of God when we love God and obey his commandments. For the love of God is this, that we keep his commandments. And his commandments are not burdensome, for whoever is begotten by God conquers the world. And the victory that conquers the world is our faith. Who indeed is the victor over the world but the one who believes that Jesus is the Son of God?

This is the one who came through water and blood, Jesus Christ, not by water alone, but by water and blood. The Spirit is the one that testifies, and the Spirit is truth.

### THIRD SUNDAY OF EASTER, April 19, 2015
*Second Reading* (1 John 2:1-5a)
My children, I am writing this to you so that you may not commit sin. But if anyone does sin, we have an Advocate with the Father, Jesus Christ the righteous one. He is expiation for our sins, and not for our sins only but for those of the whole world. The way we may be sure that we know him is to keep his commandments. Those who say, "I know him," but do not keep his commandments are liars, and the truth is not in them. But whoever keeps his word, the love of God is truly perfected in him.

### FOURTH SUNDAY OF EASTER, April 26, 2015
*Second Reading* (1 John 3:1-2)
Beloved: See what love the Father has bestowed on us that we may be called the children of God. Yet so we are. The reason the world does not know us is that it did not know him. Beloved, we are God's children now; what we shall be has not yet been revealed. We do know that when it is revealed we shall be like him, for we shall see him as he is.

### FIFTH SUNDAY OF EASTER, May 3, 2015
*Second Reading* (1 John 3:18-24)
Children, let us love not in word or speech but in deed and truth.

Now this is how we shall know that we belong to the truth and reassure our hearts before him in whatever our hearts condemn, for God is greater than our hearts and knows everything. Beloved, if our hearts do not condemn us, we have confidence in God and receive from him whatever we ask, because we keep his commandments and do what pleases him. And his commandment is this: we should believe in the name of his Son, Jesus Christ, and love one another just as he commanded us. Those who keep his commandments remain in him, and he in them, and the way we know that he remains in us is from the Spirit he gave us.

### SIXTH SUNDAY OF EASTER, May 10, 2015
*Second Reading* (1 John 4:7-10)
Beloved, let us love one another, because love is of God; everyone who loves is begotten by God and knows God. Whoever is without love does not know God, for God is love. In this way the love of God was revealed to us: God sent his only Son into the world so that we might have life through him. In this is love: not that we have loved God, but that he loved us and sent his Son as expiation for our sins.

## THE ASCENSION OF THE LORD, May 14 or 17, 2015
### Second Reading (Eph 4:1-13 [or Eph 1:17-23 or Eph 4:1-7, 11-13])

Brothers and sisters, I, a prisoner for the Lord, urge you to live in a manner worthy of the call you have received, with all humility and gentleness, with patience, bearing with one another through love, striving to preserve the unity of the spirit through the bond of peace: one body and one Spirit, as you were also called to the one hope of your call; one Lord, one faith, one baptism; one God and Father of all, who is over all and through all and in all.

But grace was given to each of us according to the measure of Christ's gift. Therefore, it says:

> He ascended on high and took prisoners captive;
> he gave gifts to men.

What does "he ascended" mean except that he also descended into the lower regions of the earth? The one who descended is also the one who ascended far above all the heavens, that he might fill all things.

And he gave some as apostles, others as prophets, others as evangelists, others as pastors and teachers, to equip the holy ones for the work of ministry, for building up the body of Christ, until we all attain to the unity of faith and knowledge of the Son of God, to mature to manhood, to the extent of the full stature of Christ.

## SEVENTH SUNDAY OF EASTER, May 17, 2015
### Second Reading (1 John 4:11-16)

Beloved, if God so loved us, we also must love one another. No one has ever seen God. Yet, if we love one another, God remains in us, and his love is brought to perfection in us.

This is how we know that we remain in him and he in us, that he has given us of his Spirit. Moreover, we have seen and testify that the Father sent his Son as savior of the world. Whoever acknowledges that Jesus is the Son of God, God remains in him and he in God. We have come to know and to believe in the love God has for us.

God is love, and whoever remains in love remains in God and God in him.

## PENTECOST SUNDAY, May 24, 2015
### Second Reading (Gal 5:16-25 [or 1 Cor 12:3b-7, 12-13])

Brothers and sisters, live by the Spirit and you will certainly not gratify the desire of the flesh. For the flesh has desires against the Spirit, and the Spirit against the flesh; these are opposed to each other, so that you may not do what you want. But if you are guided by the Spirit, you are not under the law. Now the works of the flesh are obvious: immorality, impurity, lust, idolatry, sorcery, hatreds, rivalry, jealousy, outbursts of fury, acts of selfishness, dissensions, factions, occasions of envy, drinking bouts, orgies, and the like. I warn you, as I warned you before, that those who do such things will not inherit the kingdom of God. In contrast, the fruit of the Spirit is love, joy, peace, patience, kindness, generosity, faithfulness, gentleness, self-control. Against such there is no law. Now those who belong to Christ Jesus have crucified their flesh with its passions and desires. If we live in the Spirit, let us also follow the Spirit.

## THE MOST HOLY TRINITY, May 31, 2015
### Second Reading (Rom 8:14-17)

Brothers and sisters: Those who are led by the Spirit of God are sons of God. For you did not receive a spirit of slavery to fall back into fear, but you received a Spirit of adoption, through whom we cry, "Abba, Father!" The Spirit himself bears witness with our spirit that we are children of God, and if children, then heirs, heirs of God and joint heirs with Christ, if only we suffer with him so that we may also be glorified with him.

## THE MOST HOLY BODY AND BLOOD OF CHRIST (Corpus Christi), June 7, 2015
### Second Reading (Heb 9:11-15)

Brothers and sisters: When Christ came as high priest of the good things that have come to be, passing through the greater and more perfect tabernacle not made by hands, that is, not belonging to this creation, he entered once for all into the sanctuary, not with the blood of goats and calves but with his own blood, thus obtaining eternal redemption. For if the blood of goats and bulls and the sprinkling of a heifer's ashes can sanctify those who are defiled so that their flesh is cleansed, how much more will the blood of Christ, who through the eternal Spirit offered himself unblemished to God, cleanse our consciences from dead works to worship the living God.

For this reason he is mediator of a new covenant: since a death has taken place for deliverance from transgressions under the first covenant, those who are called may receive the promised eternal inheritance.

## THE ASSUMPTION OF THE BLESSED VIRGIN MARY, August 15, 2015
### Second Reading (1 Cor 15:20-27)

Brothers and sisters: Christ has been raised from the dead, the firstfruits of those who have fallen asleep. For since death came through man, the resurrection of the dead came also through man. For just as in Adam all die, so too in Christ shall all be brought to life, but each one in proper order: Christ the firstfruits; then, at his coming, those who belong to Christ; then comes the end, when he hands over the Kingdom to his God and Father, when he has destroyed every sovereignty and every authority and power. For he must reign until he has put all his enemies under his feet. The last enemy to be destroyed is death, for "he subjected everything under his feet."

## ALL SAINTS, November 1, 2015
### Second Reading (1 John 3:1-3)

Beloved: See what love the Father has bestowed on us that we may be called the children of God. Yet so we are. The reason the world does not know us is that it did not know him. Beloved, we are God's children now; what we shall be has not yet been revealed. We do know that when it is revealed we shall be like him, for we shall see him as he is. Everyone who has this hope based on him makes himself pure, as he is pure.

### Second Reading (Rev 1:5-8)

Jesus Christ is the faithful witness, the firstborn of the dead and ruler of the kings of the earth. To him who loves us and has freed us from our sins by his blood, who has made us into a kingdom, priests for his God and Father, to him be glory and power forever and ever. Amen.

Behold, he is coming amid the clouds, / and every eye will see him, / even those who pierced him. / All the peoples of the earth will lament him. / Yes. Amen.

"I am the Alpha and the Omega," says the Lord God, "the one who is and who was and who is to come, the almighty."